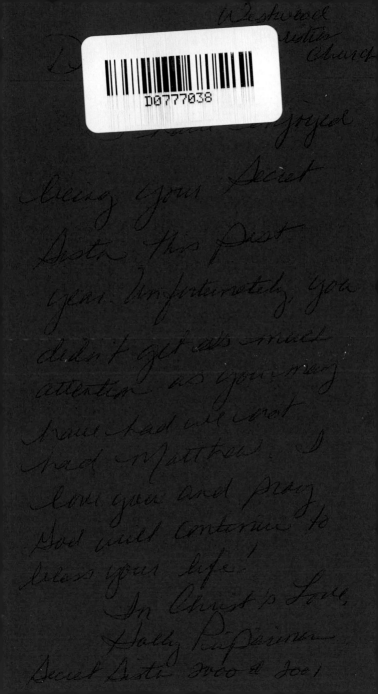

Westwood
D...............ristian Church

.... have enjoyed

being your Secret

Sister this past

year. Unfortunately, you

didn't get as much

attention as you may

have had we not

had Matthew. I

love you and pray

God will continue to

bless your life!

In Christ's Love,
Holly Purinsun

Secret Sister 2000 & 2001

"Hectic schedules and hurried relationships can crowd out the best that God intends for us. *Simply the Savior* offers a rich alternative to the pressured pace that stifles a rewarding life."

Mary White, author
Harsh Grief, Gentle Hope

"Nancy Parker Brummett draws the reader closer to the heart of God in many caring and insightful ways. Clearly, God spoke to me through *Simply the Savior*."

Roy Lessin, co-founder and
senior editor of DaySpring Cards

Simply the Savior

Nancy Parker Brummett

Chariot Victor Publishing
A Division of Cook Communications

Chariot Victor Publishing
Cook Communications, Colorado Springs, CO 80918
Cook Communications, Paris, Ontario
Kingsway Communications, Eastbourne, England

SIMPLY THE SAVIOR
© 1998 by Nancy Parker Brummett

Cover design: Bill Gray
Cover illustration: Bob de la Pena
Editor: Julie Smith

First printing, 1998
Printed in the United States of America

5 4 3 2 1 Printing/Year 02 01 00 99 98

Library of Congress Cataloging-in-Publication Data

Brummett, Nancy Parker.
      Simply the Savior: a woman's search for simple joy/Nancy Parker
Brummett
      p. cm.
ISBN 1-56476-752-3
1. Simplicity--Religious aspects--Christianity. 2. Women--Religious life. 3.
Brummett, Nancy Parker. I. Title.
BV4647.S48B78   1998   98-23393
248.8'43--dc21   CIP

CVP edition: ISBN 1-56476-752-3
BTY edition: ISBN 1-56476-759-0

Contents

Acknowledgments

My heartfelt thanks go to Phil Wilcoxson and Susan Riches at *Best to You* for believing in this project and to Karl Schaller and Julie Smith, my capable and caring editor, at Chariot Victor Publishing.

Additional thanks go to my family and my friends for their encouragement and prayers. Books are rarely written by one person. Certainly everyone who has ever touched my life in any way is a part of this one.

Praise be to our Lord Jesus Christ. Great is His faithfulness.

—N. P. B.

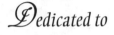

Dedicated to
my husband, Jim,
whose faithful encouragement
and support free me to become
the woman God created me to be.

—*N.P. B.*

CHAPTER 1

Simply Believe

Jesus said to her,
"I am the resurrection and the life.
He who believes in me will live, even though he dies;
and whoever lives and believes in me will never die.
Do you believe this?"
—John 11:25-26

Most of us have had enough of living in the midst of a self-made whirlwind. We desperately crave simplification and the balance and harmony it can bring to our lives.

Yet sustaining a simpler, saner life-style over time is very difficult to do. We clean out a closet and within the week it's cluttered again. We decline a request to serve on a committee one day, only to accept two more extra responsibilities the next.

How can we simplify our lives to be more serene, more focused, and more significant on a permanent basis? How can we calm the fear in our hearts that what we see of this world is all there is?

I believe that it is this fear, more than anything else, that fuels our busyness as we desperately try to control and hold on to everyone and everything we love.

I also believe that the only hope for the lasting, effective simplification of our lives is a relationship with the Savior Jesus Christ. Once He's in control we never have to fear losing control again. In Him we are found, not lost. In Him we are free, not enslaved to the demands of this world.

Mary and Martha were two sisters who lived in Bethany in the time of Jesus. When they lost their brother Lazarus their whole world was turned upside down. To be without a husband or a brother in those days meant that their very survival was at stake.

Martha rushed out to meet Jesus as He approached their home after Lazarus had died. Jesus loved His friends. When He saw the fear and panic in Martha's eyes, He quieted her spirit by saying, "I am the resurrection and the life. He who believes in me will live, even though he dies; and whoever lives and believes in me will never die. Do you believe this?" (John 11:25-26)

He asks the same question of each of us today, and nothing impacts our ability to live a simple, secure life of faith more than the answer we give Him. Yet often we're so busy trying to find reliable stepping stones on our own that we never take the leap of faith He asks us to take. This was certainly true of me.

Five months after I was officially divorced, on a hot day in June, 1982, I waved good-by to my sons in the driveway of my parents' home in Tennessee. The boys' dad met me there to pick them up for a six-week visit with him in New Jersey. I was headed back to Colorado to live all alone for the first time in my life.

Since there had been some talk about my older son staying with his dad for the next school year, I waved good-by not knowing if he would ever really be coming home again. I didn't even know what would be best for him. I just knew my whole life had fallen apart, and I still didn't understand why.

As soon as the boys were out of sight, I went in the house to change clothes. My mom asked if I was okay. "I'm fine," I lied. "I'm going for a jog."

Physical activity was one way I tried to regain control of my life that year, so within a few minutes of the boys' departure I was running around the track at my old high school in the hot summer sun. Soon uncontrollable tears mingled with the drops of sweat running down my face. I kept running, but I couldn't stop crying.

Finally, I dropped to my knees and said, "Lord, I can't do this anymore. I can't control what's happening, and even if I could, I don't know the right answers. I've made such a mess of things on my own. Please help me."

If there was one defining moment in my life when I surrendered completely to Him, that was it. From then on, I became more than a Sunday Christian. The letting go process took time, and I still find myself clinging to certain things too tightly; but since I asked for His help, I've had the assurance of the Holy Spirit reminding me that my life is in more capable hands than my own. The more I allow Jesus to be Lord of my life in every way, the better I know Him. The better I know Him, the more I desire His simple, yet gloriously satisfying, way of living.

It's too bad that it so often takes dire circumstances such as mine before we understand our need for a Savior. For many, believing in God comes more easily than accepting Jesus, and it's this belief to which they cling as they attempt to deal with life's struggles. I've even seen this tendency in women who are serious enough about their faith to be in Bible study groups. They believe in God, pray to Him, and wait patiently for His answers. Yet they are blocking His responses, perhaps even insulting Him, because they refuse to recognize His Son as Savior and Lord.

Not until we know the Son can we have full access to God's heart and find the peace that passes all understanding: the peace that comes from the assurance of eternal life.

. . . . . ❖ . . . . .

Often we're so busy trying to find reliable stepping stones on our own, we never take the leap of faith Jesus asks us to take.

. . . . . ❖ . . . . .

In John 14:6, Jesus said, "I am the way and the truth and the life. No one comes to the Father except through me. If you really knew me, you would know my Father as well." Unless, as C. S. Lewis so aptly states in *Mere Christianity*, you dismiss Jesus as a liar or a lunatic, then you have to accept what He said as God's truth.[1]

Why don't more people accept God's free gift of salvation, and claim His power to simplify their lives? Maybe it's because the simplest gifts, those most generously given, are the hardest to accept. Or maybe it's because nothing else we experience in life is so uncomplicated and unconditional.

Stand in the checkout lane at the grocery store and read the magazine covers. Count how many times you read "Ten Ways to a Younger You" or "Fifty Steps to Quicker Weight Loss." If even the simplest approach to solving one of life's dilemmas involves so many steps, how can salvation be so simple? Because God designed it that way.

In the simplest terms, Jesus came to close the gap sin created between God and us. (My sins are painfully obvious to me, but if you doubt that you are a sinner, give yourself a reality check. Read one of the Gospels and compare your life to Jesus' life on earth.) Because God is just, someone had to pay the price for sin. That someone is God's own Son, Jesus. Fully God, He also became fully human to die in our place.

There is nothing left for us to do but pick up His gift and claim it as our own, but in the skeptical world in which we live, many people can't believe the gift is real so they leave it on the shelf unclaimed. This is heartbreaking when claiming it is so easy.

All we have to do is confess our sin and our need for a Savior, believe that Jesus is the Son of God, and invite Jesus to be Lord of our lives—not just on Sunday, but every day of the week. When He becomes Lord of our whole lives, then He becomes Lord of our closets, our daily planners, our business proposals, our relationships, and our car pools. Then and only then can we tap into the power that will enable us to simplify our lives on a permanent basis.

Without Jesus standing guard over our hearts, any space we are able to create for ourselves through simplification is soon filled up with new activities and commitments. If we don't refill it ourselves, well-intentioned spouses, colleagues, or others will fill it up for us. Soon it's been reclaimed by possessions, careers, or other people's expectations of us, and we lose the balance and harmony we hoped to find.

Jesus sees the panic in our eyes. He is walking toward each one of us as He walked toward Martha on the road outside of her house. He's telling us who He is and what He was sent to do for us, and He's asking, "Do you believe this?" I'm convinced that until we can say, "I do believe," from the depths of our hearts, we will never have the power to let go of the fear, the need to be in control, that fuels so much meaningless activity.

The first step to simplifying our lives is to simply believe, and everything else will follow.

CHAPTER 2

Simply Pray

*But when you pray, go into your room,
close the door and pray
to your Father, who is unseen.*
—Matthew 6:6

Why is it that the same women who wouldn't think of leaving the house without their cell phones will forget about the one form of communication that connects them with the Lord of the Universe?

To pray is simply to have a personal conversation with your best friend. Like every conversation we have, praying is two way, and we must learn to simplify our lives so that we can pray effectively and clearly hear God's voice.

Even when He was still on earth, Jesus and the Father were one. In John 17:21 when Jesus prays for us, He asks, "That all of them may be one, Father, just as you are in me and I am in you."

In spite of this complete unity with God, Jesus always stopped to pray. He prayed early in the morning and late at night. He prayed alone on the mountain and with His disciples by the seashore. He prayed in times of temptation and trial, of course, but He also prayed in times of joy and thanksgiving. In short, He prayed at all times, because He needed and wanted to talk with His Father.

Seeing Jesus' faithfulness to prayer, the disciples asked Him how they were to pray. In Matthew 6:6 when He tells them to go into their room and pray, He encourages them to put private conversation with God ahead of appearing pious in public. Certainly Jesus prayed in public, and there are times when we are called to do so too. But the simple prayers of our hearts, in the most private chambers of our lives, are the prayers that shape us. Our private prayers add depth to our public ones.

What keeps us from praying effectively? Clutter. Just as when we go into our rooms or closets our peaceful retreat can be ruined by the sight of physical clutter, our communication with God can be muddled by the spiritual clutter in our lives.

Simplifying our lives includes getting rid of both kinds of clutter, and attacking physical clutter may be a great way to prepare for attacking the more serious kind.

The best rule I know for getting rid of clutter is the one that dictates, "If you haven't needed it in the past year, get rid of it." Certainly there are exceptions to this rule. You may not have needed the needlepoint pillow your great aunt made for you, but you're not going to give it away. But what about those slacks that will be too tight even if you do lose five pounds? What about the three cans of ground cinnamon in your kitchen cupboard? Can they be consolidated into one can? Cupboard by cupboard, closet by closet, room by room, you can unclutter your life. It's so liberating!

Now, look at your prayer life with the same discerning eye. In John 15:7, Jesus says, "If you remain in me and my words remain in you, ask whatever you wish, and it will be given you." Too often, Christians focus on the last part of this promise and overlook the initial requirement. What does Christ mean when He says we are to remain in Him? More than anything, He wants us to simply ask His will for us in every situation, and to be in intimate relationship with Him.

It's a difficult question, but sooner or later we all have to ask ourselves if the clutter keeping us from praying effectively, and keeping us from hearing God's answer to our prayers, is wrapped in a spirit of sin or unforgiveness. In James 5:16 we are promised, "The prayer of a righteous man is powerful and effective." We know "righteousness" is ours when we confess our sins and believe in Jesus as Lord. To pray effectively then, we must get rid of the clutter of sin and come to God with an open heart.

We must also come with a contrite heart.

· · · · · ❖ · · · · ·

$\mathscr{T}$o pray is simply to have a personal conversation with your best friend.

· · · · · ❖ · · · · ·

As a freelance writer, I had the privilege of working on a prayer journal for which I was asked to excerpt copy from the published works of author Evelyn Christenson. Then in her mid-seventies, Evelyn was busy touring the world holding prayer seminars and proclaiming to others the simple power of prayer. Two million copies of her best-selling book, *What Happens When Women Pray*, are in print.

Working with Evelyn was a joy and a privilege, but as happens to many of us when we over commit and over estimate the amount of discretionary time we have, I was dangerously close to missing the promised deadline on the project. Getting up before the sun one cold morning in December, 1996, I stumbled into the kitchen and put on a pot of coffee. Standing in the kitchen in my bathrobe and fuzzy slippers waiting for the coffee to brew, I leaned back against the kitchen sink, lowered my head, and prayed through my tears:

"Lord, I was so honored that You gave me this assignment, but I fear I have failed You. I wanted to thoroughly absorb every book and pray over every entry just as Evelyn would do, and I simply haven't done it. I'm sorry, Lord. This assignment is due! Please help me. Please show me what You want to include in this prayer journal. In Christ's name, amen."

Steaming cup of coffee in hand, I went back to my office and turned on the computer. I picked up the first book of Evelyn's, in which I had highlighted excerpts, and began copying her words into the new text. Then I moved on to the books I hadn't looked at carefully enough. It was as if God had taken a highlighter (I think He would use purple) to every book I picked up. As I scanned the pages, He seemed to be saying, "I want this . . . and this . . . and this paragraph, here." My work was almost done when I heard His answer to my prayer.

"Don't you see, My child," the Lord was saying to me.

"I didn't give you this assignment so you could study what happens when women pray. I gave it to you so you could learn what happens when *you* pray, and come to Me for forgiveness and help."

Just as I sensed God's answer to my prayer, I became aware of a golden glow filling every corner of my home office. I turned to see one of His most magnificent sunrises spreading across the Colorado prairie. As if God didn't feel that was quite enough confirmation that He was with me, I then turned to look out the other window in my office and saw a full moon still shining over the mountain range. God does such awesome work.

I still have a lot to learn about prayer. I still need to remember to pray first instead of after I've exhausted all other possibilities. But tenderly, time after time, the Lord keeps saying, "I'm here. I'm listening. All you have to do is ask." Simply pray, and He will hear you.

CHAPTER 3

Simply Consider

> *Consider the lilies of the field, how they grow;*
> *they toil not, neither do they spin: And yet I say unto you, That even*
> *Solomon in all his glory was not arrayed like one of these.*
> —Matthew 6:28-29 KJV

Shortly after I gave up the job that kept me away from home from pre-dawn to dusk and began working at home instead, I became aware of birds as never before. Little sparrows were playing and chirping in the bushes outside my home office window. Hawks were soaring against the blue sky above the field next to our house, playfully sailing on the currents. Even the starlings in the trees at the grocery store parking lot captured my attention.

It was quite an awakening when I realized that the birds had been a part of my world all along. I had just been too busy and distracted to notice them. Now I keep the feeders in our yard full, and I've attached feeders to my office and kitchen windows so wild birds are my constant companions. My summer friends the hummingbirds are my favorites, and their antics have even appeared in my weekly newspaper column from time to time.

If I had missed something as obviously delightful as the bird population, I wondered, what other parts of God's creation had I busily ignored? Job 12:7 says, "But ask the animals, and they will teach you, or the birds of the air, and they will tell you." I had been missing all their gentle lessons.

Fortunately, I'm blessed to live in a part of the country where it's impossible to ignore the majesty of God's Creation completely. The front range of the Rocky Mountains runs all along the west side of Colorado Springs. In the mornings, the mountains seem to glow with a pink luminescence as they reflect the sunrise. When they are covered with snow in the winter, they look like giant dollops of pink cake icing or swirls of cotton candy.

Yet even beauty as commanding as this can be dismissed with a glance when the mind and soul are otherwise engaged. After my revelation about the birds, which left me feeling as if I had just emerged from a deep coma, I made it a priority to pay more attention to the simple beauty of the natural world.

. . . . . ❖ . . . . .

His truth simplifies our lives
—and sets us free.

. . . . . ❖ . . . . .

As Christians who want to steer clear of the pantheistic worship of trees and rocks, we often stop short of applauding God for His most excellent work. We may proclaim His miraculous hand when we observe the birth of a baby, or marvel at the intricacy of a blossom, but there's so much more. All of creation is full of mysteries God wants us to discover in order to understand fully who He is and what He has given us. To do so reinforces the assurance He wants us to have that He truly will provide for our needs. To do so helps us simplify our lives as we trust Him to provide.

The best way I know to connect with God's Creation is to go on a nature walk with a small child—preferably a child short enough to notice an ant making its way down the crack in the sidewalk. If you don't have such a child in your life, borrow one! You won't regret it.

Every time my little granddaughters visit I see new

marvels through their eyes. One summer we sat in some natural sand that had been imported to create a lakeside Colorado beach. We'd been digging and playing in the sand for some time when my then five-year-old granddaughter became all excited. Holding a handful of sand up to me she said, "Look, Grancy, there's glitter in the sand!" Sure enough, some part of the ground up material contained a sparkly substance, but I never would have noticed it without her. Now the entire beach looks like a field of diamonds to me.

Author and theologian Richard J. Foster, in his book *Freedom of Simplicity,* refers to Matthew 6 as "the most radiant passage on Christian simplicity in all the Bible."[2] In this often quoted selection of Scripture, Jesus encourages us to behold the birds and how God takes care of them, reminding us that we are surely more important than they are. He urges us to consider the lilies of the field and how they grow. "They toil not, neither do they spin: And yet I say unto you, That even Solomon in all his glory was not arrayed like one of these" (Matt. 6:28-29 KJV).

It's impossible to overstate the effect taking these verses in Matthew's Gospel to heart can have on our ability to simplify our lives. As a woman, they especially speak to my desire to clothe myself in the latest styles, most flattering colors, and most sumptuous fabrics.

A few years ago I found I was suffering from a malady

that I dubbed "packaphobia." Every time I had to get ready to go on a trip, even the simplest two-day weekend, I would stand in my closet staring at my clothes without being able to choose anything. Finally forcing myself to select something (after all, planes do leave on time!), I would pack far too much and wind up taking half of what I had packed out of my bag again.

My husband began to dread going through this with me, and he knew to stay as far away from the bedroom as he could while I was packing. The night before a trip, he would tentatively ask me if I had packed, although he resorted to saying "the P word" instead of "pack" because he knew just the mention of the word itself could throw me into a tizzy.

Having read this you must think I'm totally neurotic. However, other than a touch of claustrophobia (probably caused by all that time in the closet!), I can assure you I'm virtually phobia-free.

The cause of the packaphobia was simple. I had too many clothes from which to choose. Always giving in to the impulse to buy a great silk blouse that was on sale, or a good pair of red wool slacks to have for the holidays, I had turned my wardrobe into a bargain basement where few things coordinated and even fewer had earned their right to be taking up hanger space in my closet.

Though I know my wardrobe will never consist of

just the sackcloth and rope belt of St. Francis or the simple white robes of Mother Teresa, drastic measures were called for. I began by sorting everything I owned into three piles: the "keepers," things to take to the consignment store, and items to give to charity. Sure, I changed my mind a few times, and I gave away some things I probably should have kept, but basically this procedure simplified my closet and my life.

Next, I disciplined myself to go shopping only for items I needed to fill certain spots in my wardrobe. My ultimate goal? To have a neutral-color, coordinated ensemble for each season, to include a blazer, skirt, blouse, and slacks or shorts, which I could easily grab and pack whenever a trip came up. Once the basics were in place (by the way, I consider the color red a basic), it was easy to add a vest or a scarf for variety and fun. I can't begin to tell you how healing this process was.

Soon I saw that Matthew 6 could be applied to my physical appearance in general, and that it also needed to be applied to my philosophy about aging.

I know women who have the funds and the inclination to do anything and everything to delay and disguise the effects of aging. Plastic surgery, liposuction, laser treatments—they have access to it all. Occasionally I bump into someone in the grocery store who looks a good ten years younger than the last time I saw her! Without Jesus as Lord of my life, the temptation to join their ranks would be great. No one likes crow's feet, sagging jowls, or droopy eyes, and the gray in my hair is going from subtle wisps to definite stripes.

Yet over the years I've learned I can trust God to maintain my body and my appearance along with the rest of Creation. How could I insult Him by telling Him I didn't like myself the way He created me?

When I began to agonize over whether to dye my hair, I prayed about my decision, and I meditated on 1 Peter 3:4 about a woman's true beauty being a "gentle and quiet spirit." This doesn't mean God wants us to be doormats. In the original text, the word translated as *gentle* means "meek, under authority" and the word translated as *quiet* means "full of faith."

I desire that kind of beauty, and I believe God doesn't want me spending any more energy or resources on my physical appearance than I already am. Besides, Proverbs 16:31 says, "Gray hair is a crown of splendor; it is attained by a righteous life."

I will still try to look my best, but I'd rather focus on that "gentle and quiet spirit," so I will be beautiful in the Lord's eyes—than sit in a salon waiting for a hair color to take or a set of fake nails to dry.

Framed on the wall of my home office is a calligraphic treatment of Matthew 6:28-29 with a glorious watercolor of gold and orange lilies. Daily it reminds me not to fret about my clothes and my appearance. It also reminds me not to fret about my income: God will provide for my needs as long as I simply consider His promise to care for me even as He cares for the birds at my window.

In terms of my appearance, I'm glad I gave the Master His hand, and I'm excited to see how He will fashion me inside and out in the years to come. I no longer waste time or energy trying to do His job for Him.

Simply consider what Jesus taught us when He spoke of the birds and the lilies. As always, His truth simplifies our lives—and sets us free.

CHAPTER 4

Simply Say So

Do not worry beforehand about what to say.
Just say whatever is given you at the time,
for it is not you speaking, but the Holy Spirit.
—Mark 13:11

How much simpler life is for people who say what they mean and mean what they say. How much easier it is to share our faith with others when we are bold enough to simply tell them what Jesus Christ has done for us.

One day as I drove to the automated teller machine, the Christian radio station blaring on my car radio played a particularly uplifting gospel rendition of "I Have Decided to Follow Jesus." I started singing along. After going into the ATM booth, as I waited for the machine to transact my business, I kept right on singing: "I have decided to follow Jesus. I have decided to follow Jesus. I have decided to follow Jesus. No turning back. No turning back."

Have you ever noticed how great the acoustics are in those little concrete and metal booths? Being pleased with the sound of my voice (this was even better than the shower!), I repeated the chorus—only much louder this time. I also began clapping my hands and rocking back and forth. All alone in the booth, I tossed my head back to really blast one of the high notes. That's when I spied the security camera aimed right at me.

Now I don't know who monitors those security cameras, but I immediately envisioned a whole bank full of people . . . officers negotiating loans . . . tellers cashing checks . . . at least a roomful of people working in cubicles . . . all ceasing their activity to stare at the Mahalia Jackson "wannabe" in the ATM booth.

The second I saw the camera I stopped singing, grabbed my cash and receipt, got back in my car, and drove away as quickly as I could.

Why was that my reaction? I not only agreed with the words to the song, I wanted to live them. Why wasn't I bold enough to look right into the camera, finish the chorus, and simply say, "I hope you decide to follow Him too?"

I think it's very difficult for us to share Jesus Christ with others when we don't know how He will be received. To expose ourselves to rejection is one thing. To expose the Lord of the Universe to rejection is something else again.

But hasn't He already overcome the greatest persecution and the most complete rejection anyone could ever endure? The Bible assures us that God will determine who hears and accepts His truth. We only have to be willing to say what it means to us to be followers of the Savior. Jesus Christ does not need us to defend Him, only to represent Him.

Many Christians have both public and private opportunities to share the Gospel with others. It can be intimidating for us, but it doesn't have to be.

Jesus doesn't ask us to speak up for Him and then leave us all alone. He doesn't even expect us to come up with the words alone.

In Mark 13, Jesus warns His disciples what to expect near the end times. After saying that the Gospel must be preached to all nations, He tells His faithful followers that they may be brought to trial and interrogated. "Do not worry beforehand about what to say. Just say whatever is given to you at the time, for it is not you speaking, but the Holy Spirit" (Mark 13:11).

I believe any time we are bold enough to speak the

Gospel, whether we are in a physically precarious situation or not, the Holy Spirit will help us with the words if we have prayed and turned the opportunity over to Him.

The more in touch we are with Jesus, the more often He may expect us to simply say to others what He has done for us. Stating the facts of what we know and believe to be true defuses most senseless arguments. And once the Lord decides He wants you to speak up for Him, you might as well do it. Trust me; I once had Him follow me through the streets of Salisbury, England in a red bus with a loud speaker in order to get my attention!

At the time, I was on vacation with two of my best friends. The day before the three of us had visited Avebury, the site of interesting rock formations similar to those at Stonehenge. I was concerned when I saw people celebrating the summer solstice who seemed to be praying and according power to the rocks. I wanted to tell my friends what I was feeling, but I was afraid they would think I was overreacting, so I kept quiet. As I prayed, however, the Holy Spirit began working on me. I slept restlessly all night.

The next day, we were driving through Salisbury trying to find the road leading to the cathedral, when we became aware of a red double-decker bus behind us. It wasn't just any bus. This one was playing loud, contemporary Christian music through a loud speaker. On the side was the word "Je-Bus." No one was on the bus except the driver, and the destination window above his head read "Heaven." Finally, my friend who was driving grew tired of the noise and the stares of all the people on the sidewalk who turned to gawk at us along with the bus, so she pulled over to let it pass.

I almost laughed out loud. "Lord, You really have a sense of humor," I thought. "Now You're chasing me with a bus to encourage me to be bolder in my faith. I don't know where this is going, but I'm definitely along for the ride."

· · · · · ✦ · · · · ·

Jesus Christ does not need us to defend Him, only to represent Him.

· · · · · ✦ · · · · ·

At last we located the pedestrian walkway leading to the Salisbury Cathedral, parked the car, and walked through a centuries-old stone arch. I glanced to my right to see this verse from the Gospel of John in four-inch letters on the wall: "And this is life eternal, that they might know thee the only true God, and Jesus Christ, whom thou hast sent" (John 17:3 KJV).

A few steps farther along I was drawn to a simple plaque honoring three Christian martyrs burned at the stake on that site. "Nice touches, Lord," I said quietly. "First You send a bus playing Christian music, then You give me this Scripture, and follow up with a reminder that many believers have been persecuted in Your name. What is it I'm afraid of again?"

Later, while waiting for our meal at the pub across from the cathedral, I finally mustered the courage to bring up my feelings about Avebury.

"I need to talk about something," I began, "and I have to trust that our friendship is strong enough for you to listen without condemning me for my beliefs, even if they aren't exactly like your own."

My friends assured me it was.

"I need for you to understand what I was feeling yesterday," I continued. "It made me incredibly sad to see that there are people who, when they could be worshiping the Almighty God of the Universe, choose to worship rocks instead. I enjoyed the beauty around us yesterday, too, but rocks can't bring healing or forgiveness. Only God can, through His Son Jesus Christ."

We talked for several minutes, until our dinner was served. Finally the knot in my stomach was gone because, through the Holy Spirit, the Lord had given me the courage and the words to say what I believed. Now I can remember Avebury not as the site of pagan rituals, but as a monument to His faithfulness.

Toward the end of each school year, the teenagers who have been gathering on Monday nights for Young Life Club have what they call a "say so." At a "say so," young people who feel so moved stand up to simply share what the Lord has done in their lives.

Why should our attempts to share the Gospel be any more complicated? As it says in 1 Peter 3:15, we need to be ready to share a message of hope with others "with gentleness and respect." Like the women who visited the tomb after Jesus' resurrection, then hurried away "afraid, yet filled with joy" to share the good news (Matt. 28:8), so we must be ready to tell what He has done for us.

If Jesus is Lord of your life, simply say so.

CHAPTER 5

Simply
Say No

Simply let your "Yes" be "Yes,"
and your "No," "No";
anything beyond this comes from the evil one.
—Matthew 5:37

A plate of warm, home-baked, chocolate chip cookies sat on the kitchen counter, just waiting for us to finish our dinner and dive into them. I made the cookies because my son and his family were visiting for the weekend and I wanted my granddaughters to have a special treat.

During the meal, Francesca, six, squirmed in her chair and picked at her food (probably because of the popcorn I gave her earlier in the afternoon).

"Dad, may I have a cookie?" she asked as I cleared away the plates.

"No, honey," my son answered. "You didn't eat your dinner. No dessert."

I think I was more disappointed than Francesca, but I didn't say a word. She immediately accepted her dad's decision as final. No whining. No begging. No cajoling. Just acceptance.

Watching my granddaughter's reaction, I realized what security she finds in her dad's definitive answers to her requests. I also remembered those times when she and her younger sister, Amanda, danced around saying, "Dad said yes! Dad said yes!" Their joy came from their trust that a yes from their dad was as good as gold.

Our Lord wants us to have that same security and joy when we look to Him for a yes or no answer to all of life's choices. In fact, it's impossible to live a simpler life unless we take Jesus' admonition to the disciples in Matthew 5:37 to heart: "Simply let your 'Yes' be 'Yes,' and your 'No,' 'No'; anything beyond this comes from the evil one."

Certainly living in clouds of ambivalence and confusion leaves us susceptible to Satan's lies and schemes. If he can fill up our calendars with useless activities, he can keep us from doing any kingdom work here on earth. If he can convince us that our jobs are more important than our families, he can completely destroy our society.

The temptation to say yes to everything is continuously fueled by our basic needs to be needed and to be liked. Jesus knew every temptation we know, including the temptation to say yes. In Matthew chapter four, we read about His forty days in the desert, where the Devil tried to convince Him to abandon His heavenly assignment and settle for earthly rewards instead. Not to be fooled, Jesus answered no convincingly by quoting Scripture.

In his book, *In the Name of Jesus,* theologian Henri Nouwen encourages all those going into the ministry as a profession, and even those of us just wanting to know God's will for our lives, to simply follow Jesus' lead when we're faced with the temptation to say yes.

"Look at Jesus," Nouwen writes. "The world did not pay any attention to him. He was crucified and put away. His message of love was rejected by a world in search of power, efficiency, and control."[3]

Power, efficiency, and control. How many of the things we do are motivated by a desire for one of these? How often do we simply bounce from one demand to the next because we want to be important or popular by the world's standards? Yet Jesus said no to these temptations, and we can, too, with His help.

"The long painful history of the Church is the history of people ever and again tempted to choose power over love, control over the cross, being a leader over being led.

Those who resisted this temptation to the end and thereby give us hope are the true saints," Nouwen continues.[4]

Just as we can't permanently clear the clutter from our lives without letting Jesus guard our hearts, so we can't say no with conviction unless we say yes to something more important first. When we allow Jesus to help us draw up our list of long-term goals, these goals become a screen through which every commitment and decision must pass. When we say yes to Him first, it's easier to say no to others later.

Learning to say no is one of those skills that grows stronger with practice. We can begin by saying no to things we really don't want to do but are doing through a false sense of obligation. We can then look at every commitment we've made, cancel any appointments we don't have to keep, and resign from any organizations whose meetings we dread.

Some advocates of simplification suggest that, in self defense, we should also develop lies or "prevarications" to help us escape commitments we don't want to make. But while we need to be tactful, we don't have to be dishonest. With our eyes on the Lord, we can successfully avoid committing to things we don't need to do and keep our integrity in tact. Jesus will never ask us to perjure ourselves in order to simplify our lives.

After all, I respond positively to someone telling me

she is trying to simplify her life in order to have more time with her family, and I expect you do, too. I have never bristled when someone said, "I'm trying to focus on some special goals right now, so I don't have time to do that." Instead of thinking less of such people, we respect them.

· · · · · ❖ · · · · ·

When we say yes to Jesus first, it's easier to say no to others later.

· · · · · ❖ · · · · ·

Like many women, my desire to please others can be a detriment to saying no and meaning it. It's relatively easy to say no to illegal or immoral activities—that's not the problem. The problem is saying yes to too many good things because we haven't stayed focused on our reasons for saying no.

"The enemy of the 'best' is often the 'good,'" Stephen Covey states in his best-selling book, *The Seven Habits of Highly Effective People.*[5] We need to remember that when we're faced with deciding which good things we simply have to say no to.

While refusing to add more good things to an already full list, we can learn to say no graciously. Covey quotes this excuse a friend of his wife's gave for not serving on a committee: "Sandra, that sounds like a wonderful project, a really worthy undertaking. . . . For a number of reasons, I won't be participating myself, but I want you to know how much I appreciate your invitation."[6]

How masterful. How focused. How effective.

Knowing my own weaknesses, I've found it really helps to establish personal policies to fortify me for those times when I'm tempted to say yes to an expenditure of funds or time. One of my personal policies is not to accept solicitations over the phone. Inevitably, the telemarketers call just as my husband and I are sitting down to dinner.

"Oh, I'm sorry," I say. "We have a family policy not to take telephone solicitations. Thanks, anyway." Then I hang up. Sometimes the request is for a cause I want to support, but a policy is a policy, and I can always find another way to contribute.

Another policy that has helped me simplify my life is to refuse to say yes to anything requiring my time until I've had a chance to think about how it either fits into or detracts from my long-term goals. Voice mail helps me enforce this policy, since I can mull over my response to the request before answering. (Saying no to answering the phone just because it's ringing is another great simplification technique that helps us keep control of the day.)

When I first began working as a free-lance writer, I was in the will-write-for-food mode, and I accepted any and every assignment that came along. Eventually, I began to see that there will always be more work down the road, that the Lord truly will compensate for my decreased income through my husband's work, and that He wants me to use more discretion about which assignments to accept.

Believers have the best time management tool imaginable at their disposal all the time—prayer. Many of us are turned off by Christians whose pat response to even the smallest request is, "I'll pray about it and get back to you." However, it is certainly right and good for us to pray about any decision that will require a significant amount of our time, talents, or finances—and to listen for the answer. No one is more prepared to help us sort out our priorities than Jesus.

The next time you're faced with too many good things to do, pray about it. Sleep on it. Ask the Lord to put His hand over yours as you go over the list. Trust Him to mark out the things you don't need to do, and to write in those things He wants you to do that you may not even know about yet. Then accept Jesus' power to "let your 'Yes' be 'Yes,' and your 'No,' 'No'"(Matt. 5:37).

The Apostle Paul in his letter to Titus says, "For the grace of God that brings salvation has appeared to all men. It teaches us to say 'No' to ungodliness and worldly passions, and to live self-controlled, upright and godly lives in this present age, while we wait for the blessed hope—the glorious appearing of our great God and Savior, Jesus Christ" (Titus 2:11-13).

He's our source for security and joy—and our only hope for simply saying no with conviction.

CHAPTER 6

Simply Seek

Ask and it will be given to you;
seek and you will find;
knock and the door will be opened to you.
—Matthew 7:7

I could see my breath as I trudged down the hill in the pre-dawn light on a frosty morning in February to meet my friend Merrilee. It was only 6:00 A.M., but it was the only time we could walk together.

Just over a month before, her sixteen-year-old son had died in a dune buggy accident in California. She needed to talk, and I wanted to listen. Although I didn't have the answers to her questions, I knew Jesus did. I believed

His promise that "where two or three come together in my name, there am I with them" (Matt. 18:20). I figured if I could just force myself to get out of bed and show up, He would be there walking through the cold morning mist beside us. And He would bring the answers.

As I approached the corner where we agreed to meet, I saw Merrilee already waiting there. We gave one another a parka-padded hug and set out down the sidewalk. Three steps into our walk she asked, "Why do *you* think God let this happen?"

"Here we go, Lord," I remember thinking. "I'm glad You're awake this morning, because I'm not sure I am."

Merrilee was desperately seeking God with an intensity I have never seen in anyone before or since. Instead of bitterly turning her back on Him, she wanted to be in His face—to ask Him the hard questions. She wanted to let Him know both how angry she was with Him and how much she needed Him to comfort her. With her hands firmly entrenched in the pockets of her parka and her ski hat pulled down over her ears, she set a pace that left me struggling to keep up. It was as if she thought we might catch up with God around the next corner if only we walked a little faster.

Week by week, I saw God respond to Merrilee's anguished search. She didn't get all her questions answered, but in time she accepted His grace as being sufficient for each day. Her life will never be the same, but she's been able to move on in faith.

Watching Merrilee go through this I learned how very approachable God is. He wants nothing more than to have an ongoing, close relationship with each of us, and He honors every attempt we make to be in His presence— even the desperate ones. To ensure we would always have a way to see Him, and to reach out to Him, He sent us a Savior. One who promised, "Ask and it will be given to you; seek and you will find; knock and the door will be opened to you" (Matt. 7:7).

We can't experience God, and His will for our lives, if we aren't regularly seeking Him. Satan conspires to keep us so busy we have no time for learning God's perspective on a situation before making decisions. As always, Jesus provides the perfect model for us, as He encourages us to seek the Father's will in all things. "If you knew me, you would know my Father also," He said in John 8:19. In Matthew's Gospel, when Jesus was teaching about wants and needs, He encouraged those listening to "Seek first his kingdom and his righteousness, and all these things will be given to you as well" (Matt. 6:33).

So how can we simply seek God? In his well-loved Bible study course, *Experiencing God*, Henry T. Blackaby maintains that in the present time God primarily speaks to His people by the Holy Spirit through the Bible, prayer, circumstances, and the church.[7]

I was thirty-four years old before I joined my first Bible study. Growing up in a traditional church setting, I had preconceived ideas about Bible studies being for little old ladies only—sort of one step away from an old-fashioned quilting bee or sewing circle.

. . . . . ❖ . . . . .

Because we're connected as God's created people, what one person experiences enriches the spiritual walk of others.

. . . . . ❖ . . . . .

After my divorce, a co-worker left a note on my desk quoting from Jeremiah 29:11-13: "For I know the plans I have for you," declares the Lord, "plans to prosper you and not to harm you, plans to give you hope and a future. . . . You will seek me and find me when you seek me with all your heart." The note also invited me to join a Bible study that was meeting over the lunch hour in our office building. Imagine that! People I admired were taking time out in the middle of the week to search God's Word and apply it to their daily lives. And they were praying for one another too. What a concept!

Opening God's Word on a regular basis is one of the best ways we have to "simply seek" Him and His will for our lives. Listening to the insights and experiences of other believers strengthens our own faith, but it isn't necessary to be part of a group to open the Bible and read it. A cup of coffee, my Bible, the Lord, and me make for a perfect quiet time.

We find God through prayer. I'm not a faithful journal keeper, but I know others who use prayer journals to record prayer requests and answers to prayer. By doing this, they can quickly review how God has responded to them over time. Just journaling thoughts and questions to God is a way to seek Him, too. If you keep a journal, don't bind it with shoulds. Write in it whenever and wherever you can. Keep it by your bed or in the glove compartment of the car. God will honor your attempt to seek Him.

We find God in circumstances. I knew Merrilee was seeking God on our early morning walks, but I didn't realize I would also see more of His heart through her. Because we're connected as God's created people, what one person experiences enriches the spiritual walk of others.

And we find God through church and the fellowship with other believers as we learn to use our own gifts as part of the body of Christ.

When I really know God is speaking to me is when I hear the same message two or three different ways. It's not at all uncommon for me to hear a Scripture verse I never really heard before quoted on the Christian radio station, come across it "randomly" in my morning quiet time, then arrive at church on Sunday only to find out it's the theme for the sermon! (I'm sure God must speak in much subtler ways to those who pay closer attention than I do.)

The fellowship of believers is a joy not to be missed, but those who proclaim the great outdoors is their cathedral have a valid point. It is true that we can find God by being aware of the mysteries and glories of His creation all around us. Barbara Mouser, in her study course *Five Aspects of Woman: A Biblical Theology of Femininity*, writes, "This world is the gateway to God. One reason God did not immediately say, 'look at Me,' is that we cannot immediately look at Him. He is too vast. He created this world so that by learning about this world, we would have little gateways to Him. The gateway of light, of water, of bread, of human love, of the many, many metaphors. We won't know what the Bible is talking about if we don't know something of the world."[8]

We don't need to enroll in a three-day seminar or a four-year seminary to seek God. He's all around us, and He has given us Jesus to lead us to Him.

In His beautiful prayer for all believers, Jesus prays, "Righteous Father, though the world does not know you, I know you, and they know that you have sent me. I have made you known to them, and will continue to make you known in order that the love you have for me may be in them and that I myself may be in them" (John 17:25-26).

Spend a few quiet moments in prayer. Jot a few thoughts in a journal. Study a baby's smile, or the tiny petals in the middle of a rose.

Simply seek God, and you will find Him.

CHAPTER 7

*S*imply *L*isten

*My sheep listen to my voice;
I know them, and they follow me.
I give them eternal life, and they shall never perish;
no one can snatch them out of my hand.*
—John 10:27-28

Watching the coverage of the winter Olympics, I was amazed at the courage of the jumpers in the women's freestyle aerial ski event. Spiraling sixty to seventy feet over the snow, they tucked, twisted, and turned before landing.

One young Canadian jumper had the misfortune of seeing the two competitors ahead of her take horrifying spills. Then it was her turn. While she was still in midair, the clear, strong voice of her coach calling out, "You're good! You're good! You're good!" rose above the shouts of hundreds of spectators. Hearing the voice she trusted so completely gave the ski jumper the confidence to follow through to a flawless landing.

That's what Jesus offers to do for us when we listen to His encouraging voice. Life is anything but simple if we try to respond to all the voices calling out to us at once. Yet His directions are always clear, always exactly what we need to hear in order to make it through any situation in which we find ourselves.

Jesus often described Himself as the Good Shepherd. He says, "My sheep listen to my voice; I know them, and they follow me. I give them eternal life, and they shall never perish; no one can snatch them out of my hand" (John 10:27-28).

In biblical times, sheep from different flocks often grazed together, so when a shepherd wanted his flock to move on he called out to them. Always, the sheep responded to the voice of the one who fed them, cared for them, healed their wounds, and led them to cool waters—and to that voice only. So must we respond to Jesus.

In order to be sure we are hearing His voice clearly in all circumstances, we must hear it often enough to recognize it. Like the sheep, we can then respond with confidence, knowing without a doubt that it is our Shepherd who is calling us by name (John 10:3).

When we hear a close friend misquoted, we might respond, "That doesn't sound like her." In the same way, our best defense against false messages is to develop discernment about what does and doesn't sound like Jesus.

It's not always easy. We want to follow our Shepherd, and Him only. Yet Satan is adept at delivering messages that sound amazingly close to the instructions Jesus has given us. New age spiritualists, cultists, and false teachers may also present positive messages that share common elements with Jesus' teachings, but without His grace, His mercy, and His sacrifice leading to eternal life.

The only way to truly know Jesus' voice is to listen to it. Like Mary of Bethany, we have to sit "at the Lord's feet listening" at every opportunity (Luke 10:39). We do this through reading in the Bible what Jesus said to those closest to Him, praying to Him, and spending time with Him. There are no shortcuts.

When we listen to Jesus, we'll hear Him telling us to listen to others too. Part of what it means to "lay down our life" (John 15:13) for others is to set aside our needs, and our agendas, and to listen to others without thinking about what we plan to say next. To see Jesus in other people, to understand them, to learn how we might nurture and care for them, we must first listen.

Mother Teresa told of a group of workers whose main task was to visit with the elderly. The workers were to "let them talk and talk to give them the satisfaction of being listened to." It didn't particularly matter whether what the seniors had to say was important in the world's eyes. "To listen to someone who has no one to listen to him is a very beautiful thing," Mother Teresa continued.[9]

. . . . . ❖ . . . . .

*When we listen to Jesus,
we'll hear Him telling us
to listen to others too.*

. . . . . ❖ . . . . .

Listening can also be an amazing gift to the listener. Several years ago I was inspired to launch a writing project I titled *Women Closer to the Vine.* Based on the concept in the fifteenth chapter of John's Gospel that we are all pruned as we go through life, I decided women of faith in their eighties and nineties would have been pruned a lot, and so would be living closer to the vine—closer to Jesus. I wanted their knowledge and insight.

A friend at work told me of a black woman in his church he thought I should interview: a ninety-year-old

great-grandmother who still played the piano and sang.
Before she had a stroke and could no longer recognize me,
I visited Ruth several times. Seated at her kitchen table
with a cup of coffee and a piece of fresh-baked gingerbread
or sweet potato pie in front of me, I listened as she talked
about her life.

Ruth told me about her father calling her over to his
deathbed when she was just fourteen. "Promise me I'll see
you in heaven," he said. "Do you promise?" She said, "Yes,
Daddy, I promise." She told me about all her children and
grandchildren, and about a premature baby that died in
spite of the doctor putting him in the oven to warm him
up. She told me about sixty-five years of marriage to a man
who needed a great deal of Ruth's forgiveness, and of how
by the grace of God she found it in her heart to give it to
him before he died.

"I'm not telling you any of this so you'll feel sorry for
me," Ruth said. "I'm telling you so you'll see how the Lord
protected me through it all, don't you see? I don't know
where I'd be if it weren't for the good Lord."

On my last visit to Ruth's, she turned off the gospel
music she played on her tape player night and day and
played the piano for me instead. She gave me candy to take
home, and hugs, and the benefit of a lifetime of wisdom
and prayer. She also gave me a level of understanding
about what it means to be black that I never got from

being born and raised in the South.

"I have a neighbor across the street who comes over to help me with things when my family's not around," Ruth said. "He's white, but he's real nice."

With that one statement, I saw the world through black eyes for the first time. That was a gift I would never have received had I not been willing to listen.

We benefit from listening to the Savior and from listening to all those He puts in our lives—especially our spouses, children, friends, and co-workers. In James 1:19, we're instructed to be "quick to listen," not quick to have our turn to speak.

We also benefit from listening to the Holy Spirit—the one Jesus sent to us from the Father to guide us into all truth. While we might like to think the Holy Spirit will talk to us in a booming voice like the ski coach at the Olympics, that isn't the case. Not until we have simplified our lives and turned off the noise around us will we consistently hear the still, quiet voice of Him who counsels us, corrects us, and restores our soul.

"The voice of the Spirit is as gentle as a zephyr," Oswald Chambers writes in his classic devotional *My Utmost for His Highest*, "so gentle that unless you are living in perfect communion with God, you never hear it."[10]

Fortunately, I've found the Spirit is also persistent. He may speak softly, but He'll keep speaking until even those of us not in perfect communion finally get the message. Thanks to the Spirit's leading, I'm now in a weekly Bible study with a single mom at a non-profit residential facility for single moms and their kids. Wanting to thank the Lord for protecting me and my sons through my own seven years as a single mom, I thought about volunteering there for months, but the right time never presented itself.

One day as I was driving by the big stone house, a voice in my head that I knew belonged to the Spirit said, "You can go now, or you can go later, but you're going." I turned into the parking lot and went into the house, not sure what I would say to the agency director who greeted me. After I stammered that I would be willing to lead a Bible study, he said matter-of-factly, "Oh, sure. We've been praying somebody would come." That's how the powerful Spirit clarifies priorities.

Simply listen. Listen to Jesus when He calls you by name. Listen to those He puts in your life. Listen to the Spirit who gently, persistently directs you. Simply listen, and life will be so much sweeter.

$\mathcal{S}$imply $\mathcal{T}$rust

Do not let your hearts be troubled.
Trust in God; trust also in me.
—John 14:1

There's a team-building exercise that became popular in corporate training circles several years ago. In this exercise, all the members of a given staff, or "team," stand together in a circle. Team members take turns moving to the center of the circle where they are blindfolded. They then start falling, trusting that no matter which way they fall, someone on the team will catch them before they hit the ground.

This is all well and good. It's positive and productive

to be able to trust the people with whom we spend eight or more hours a day. However, if we put our trust only in other people, sooner or later we're going to hit the ground hard.

The only One worthy of our complete trust is God: God the Father, God the Son, and God the Holy Ghost. Jesus said, "Do not let your hearts be troubled. Trust in God; trust also in me" (John 14:1). Since Jesus Christ is the same yesterday and today and forever (Heb. 13:8), His promises to us never change. Once we invite Him into our lives, we can always trust Him not to let us fall. No matter what happens to us on earth, we're eternally protected.

It's easy to trust the Lord in the good times. When there's sufficient income to pay all the bills, when the tests come back negative, when babies are born without birth defects, how simple it is to believe that He is in control and He's taking care of everything.

It's harder to trust Him when bad things happen. As I was writing about the training exercise at the beginning of this chapter I reached for the phone to call my good friend Courtney. He was the corporate trainer at the company where I worked. I wanted to check with him to make sure I remembered the exercise correctly. For a fleeting moment I imagined our conversation. We'd talk about the training exercise, laugh over a few shared memories, then move on to what really mattered most: our families, our faith.

I wanted to talk to Courtney, but I couldn't. In August, 1997 Courtney died in a fiery automobile crash. He left behind a wife, two stepsons, and a one-year-old son, all still missing his incredible zeal for life and his love. He was forty-three.

The memorial service for Courtney was an amazing testimony to the way he lived his life for others and for Jesus. Even so, there were many whys expressed. Why should Courtney's son never know what a wonderful dad he had? Why were Courtney's plans to create a Christian team-building program left unfinished? Why did such a good man die so young? Why, Lord? The answer to our questions was printed on the cover of the program for the service: "Trust in the Lord with all your heart and lean not on your own understanding" (Prov. 3:5).

Real trust is believing in God even in the midst of the whys. Trusting in His promises. Trusting in the character of God as our sovereign, omnipotent, wise, and loving Lord. Trusting, like Paul in 2 Corinthians 12:9, that His grace will be sufficient for us in every situation.

Author Linda Dillow tells of being devastated over conditions resulting from her married daughter's struggle with epilepsy. As a Christian and a missionary, Linda knew much about trusting God. As a mother, she just wanted to be able to fix things.

Finally, she found peace by focusing on the truth

that, "No difficulty, no pain, no trial that happens to me or my daughter is by chance. There are no accidents, no mistakes, no miscalculations. All is under His sovereign control. Therefore I can trust Him with my tiniest doubt or my most heart-wrenching fear. I can trust Him with what is dearest to my heart, my daughter."[11]

· · · · · ❖ · · · · ·

Jesus taught us the only good hands to be in are God's hands.

· · · · · ❖ · · · · ·

The ability to trust like this develops through time spent in relationship with God, and through prayer. Trust is strengthened when, like David in 1 Chronicles 16:12, we "Remember the wonders he has done." Trusting God in times of crisis will come more easily if we've learned to trust Him with all the less important circumstances of our lives.

For example, do we really trust Him to provide for our needs, or are we storing up lots of extra stuff just in case? Do we trust Him to help us distinguish our needs from our wants? Our lives will be so much simpler if we can simply trust.

Author E. B. White wrote an amusing but convicting

account of our inevitable accumulation of stuff:

> *I have no sharp taste for acquiring things, but it is not necessary to desire things in order to acquire them. Goods and chattels seek a man out; they find him even though his guard is up. Books and oddities arrive in the mail. Gifts arrive on anniversaries and fete days. Veterans send ball-point pens. Banks send memo books. If you happen to be a writer, readers send whatever may be cluttering up their own lives; I had a man once send me a chip of wood that showed the marks of a beaver's teeth. Someone dies, and a little trickle of indestructible keepsakes appears, to swell the flood. This steady influx is not counterbalanced by any comparable outgo. Under ordinary circumstances, the only stuff that leaves a home is paper trash and garbage; everything else stays on and digs in.*[12]

Whenever I meet a woman who seems intent on collecting more stuff, I begin to suspect she is desperate to fill an emptiness inside. There is, as the seventeenth century mathematician Pascal said, a "God-shaped hole" inside each of us that only God can fill. One reason for compulsive acquisition is the fruitless attempt to fill the hole with something besides God.

Of course, some procurement is necessary. I do

believe there's even something innate and wholesome about a woman's desire to shop, and I endorse shopping in moderation. But when I read of women who run up enormous bills shopping all day every day, or who have to have new closets built to store clothes and shoes they haven't even worn, I know there's a problem.

The major difference between houses built now and those built thirty-five years ago is the size of the closets. To compensate for the American addiction to acquire, we've opted for less living space and more storage space.[13] That says a great deal about our priorities, doesn't it?

Again, over acquisition comes down to our inability to differentiate needs from wants. "To have what we want is riches," George MacDonald wrote, "but to be able to do without is power."[14]

When I left my full-time job to begin free-lance writing at home, I knew I was going to have to adjust my spending commensurately. E.B. White would be absolutely amazed at the influx of catalogs coming into my home! I could justify receiving so many offers because, as an employee of a direct mail company, I needed them for research. I didn't need to order from them anymore, however, so I had to stop looking at them altogether in order to avoid the temptation. Now, after my period of self-imposed abstinence, I can look at catalogs again without desiring to order things I don't really need.

How was I able to go "cold turkey" on catalog shopping? I prayed about it. I asked the Lord to take away my desire to acquire, and to replace it with the satisfaction that only He can provide. He was glad to fill my order. (Free shipping and handling too!) It's true that contentment comes not to those whose means are great, but to those whose needs (and wants) are few.

Sellers of insurance or home security systems recognize that trust is so desirable that it's marketable. Have you ever noticed how often advertisers play off our need to feel safe and secure? A very clever insurance spot on television begins with a car in distress pulling off to the side of the road. A man and woman get out of the car to inspect the damage as the announcer says, "Some of us know it will be all right even when bad things happen, because we have someone to help see us through it."

The viewer assumes the next comments are coming from the man and woman, the camera pulls back to reveal two deer discussing their near collision with the car.

"Be careful," one cautions. "Where there's one, there's usually another." The deer then safely leap across the road, as the announcer says, "Being in good hands is the only place to be."™[15]

That's truth in advertising, but it has nothing to do with insurance. Jesus taught us that the only good hands to be in are God's hands. Simply trust.

CHAPTER 9

Simply Forgive

Forgive, and you will be forgiven.
—Luke 6:37

There is some more sorting and tossing that needs to be done if we are to live a life of simple freedom, and that's the cleaning out of any grudges and regrets, any unforgiven sins we are closeting.

Once again, when we turn to Jesus for help in ridding our lives of these burdens He gives us direct, straightforward instruction: "Forgive, and you will be forgiven" (Luke 6:37).

Perhaps few other realms of the human experience more quickly point out our inadequacy when compared to

SIMPLY the SAVIOR

the Savior than does the task of forgiveness. To forgive the slights, the unintentional hurts, the thoughtless acts—sure, we can do that. But He forgives us anything. Can we forgive even the more grievous sins of others? Can we forgive ourselves? And whether it is the sin of others or of ourselves that we forgive, can we rid our hearts and minds of the clutter of sin by forgetting as well as forgiving?

Jesus was perfectly clear on the issue of forgiveness. He knew that tending bitterness and cultivating grudges would take His disciples away from the more important work He had for them to do, so He frequently reminded them to forgive. He wants us to do the same.

The full impact of forgiveness comes into focus for me when I see it in others—especially in those we tend to think should not be expected to forgive.

Jerry and Mary White's son Steve, thirty years old, was senselessly murdered late one night in 1990 as he drove the taxi cab that provided additional income for the outgoing radio personality and his wife. With a motive still undetermined, the assailant shot Steve three times in the back of the head.

In Mary White's book, *Harsh Grief, Gentle Hope,* the grief-stricken mother recounts the horror of getting the news of Steve's death. The call came one morning in Columbus, Ohio where the couple was preparing to conduct a seminar in conjunction with Jerry's duties as leader of the worldwide Navigators ministry.

Mary's first whispered prayers to God began, "It can't be true. There must be some mistake. I must still be sleeping. I'll wake up now. Oh dear God, please. Please. Please don't let it be true. Let it be a dream."[16]

I clearly remember seeing the news accounts of Steve's murder on television in Colorado Springs. The senselessness and brutality of the crime shocked our mid-sized city, especially the Christian community.

When I read of the release of Mary's book in 1995, I immediately picked up a copy of it. As the mother of two sons near Steve's age when he died, I still can't read any part of that book without sobbing. Page after page, Mary tells of the agony of the days that followed the murder, then moves the reader, with her, toward the hope and healing that can only come from the Lord.

Reading the book, I was amazed and encouraged by the strength of Jerry and Mary White's faith, but the word forgiveness never occurred to me. How could a crime so horrible be forgiven?

Yet I've spoken with Mary White, and she told me that she and her husband know they have no choice but to forgive. They accept that God is the ultimate judge, and that regardless of what happens to the man who murdered their son, only forgiveness frees them from the hold the crime has over them.

Only Jesus Christ can give us the power for that kind of forgiveness. He asked His father to forgive His own murderers with His dying gasps, and He is giving these parents the strength to forgive their son's murderer. He is also freeing them from the burdens of hate and unforgiveness in the process.

Forgiveness in situations like the one the Whites face seems impossible—but all things are possible with God. It can also seem impossible to forgive ourselves for the sins we commit, especially when those sins hurt the people we love most in the world, but we must do it.

Thirteen years after my divorce, after seven years as a single mom and six years as the happily remarried mom of our new blended family, I began to feel a heaviness I had never experienced before. Through all those years I had been moving closer and closer to the Lord. I truly believed in His grace and His forgiveness, but in my heart, I never felt they included me.

"Isn't it wonderful," I would think to myself. "Look how free all those Christian people are now that their sins are forgiven. God is good indeed."

Eventually, I began to pray that God would allow me to feel in my heart the forgiveness that I knew in my head He wanted me to have. I didn't realize what that prayer would mean until I began living with an oppression like none I had ever known.

Day and night I sensed tears ready to spill over for no apparent reason. I couldn't sleep, and I felt weighed down with a tremendous weight. Like reruns of bad movies, memories of sins . . . real and imagined . . . filled my head. One by one the rationalizations and justifications for past sins, which had served me so well for years, were stripped away. I was left feeling the full burden of every selfish, thoughtless act I had ever committed.

. . . . . ❖ . . . . .

$\mathscr{J}$esus doesn't just forgive our sin, He takes away the guilt of it too.

. . . . . ❖ . . . . .

The Bible tells us all sin is equally detestable in God's eyes because it separates us from Him, but it was hard for me to understand why the memory of nights I had served warmed-over pizza to the boys for dinner were dredged up right along with acts contributing to the downfall of my first marriage. Yet any and every sin I had been closeting was displayed for my full review and confession during that time.

My husband and I sat up at night and talked, and he counseled me and held me as I sobbed and tried to understand what was happening. On a visit to Tennessee, my younger sister and I went for a long walk, and I told her what I was feeling.

"I don't understand," I said. "Why is God convicting me so harshly now when I'm so happy, and my life is going so well?"

"Because He knew you couldn't handle it earlier," was her sage reply.

After weeks of this oppression, as quickly as it descended upon me the cloud was lifted. I awoke one morning with the memory of a vision of Jesus Christ in my head. He was holding a large pair of scissors, and in front of Him was stretched a wide, pink ribbon, like the ones at ribbon-cutting ceremonies. His message to me was clear.

"It's over. I am going to cut this ribbon now," He said, "and when I do, all your past sins will be gone forever. Never dwell on them again."

In Psalm 32:4-5, David exclaims, "For day and night your hand was heavy upon me; my strength was sapped as in the heat of summer. Then I acknowledged my sin to you and did not cover up my iniquity. I said, 'I will confess my transgressions to the LORD'—and you forgave the guilt of my sin."

When I read those verses, I knew they described my own experience perfectly. In my Bible, I've underlined the word *guilt* twice. He didn't just forgive my sin, he took away the guilt of it too. It was the guilt that kept me from truly feeling forgiven all those years. Now that it was gone along with the sin, I felt a hundred pounds lighter. How much easier it has been to move forward without dragging the heavy burden of past sin behind me. That the Lord loved me enough to convict me and free me is an amazing gift of grace that will illuminate all the remaining days of my life.

Perhaps because of my encounters with Him, I love reading Jesus' encounters with women in the Bible. One day I saw His parting words to two women in a new light.

After Jesus' encounter with the woman caught in adultery, He says, "Go now and leave your life of sin" (John 8:11). After His encounter with the sinful woman who poured perfume on His feet and then wiped them with her hair, Jesus says, "Your faith has saved you; go in peace" (Luke 7:50).

Rather than research origins of the words used, or engage in any other analysis of these passages and their different authors, I decided to let them speak to me just as they were. The message was a simple one. In a sense, Jesus was telling both women the same thing; when we go and sin no more, we will also have peace.

A bumper sticker I like reads: Christians aren't perfect—just forgiven. Although it disappoints me, I know I will sin many more times before I die. My peace comes from knowing I don't have to carry the weight of future sins any longer than it takes for them to push me down to my knees in prayer.

I'm motivated to give my sin to God as soon as possible because the Bible says that God removes our sin as far as the east is from the west (Ps. 103:12). As if that still isn't far enough, He also forgets our sin (Is. 43:25; Jer. 31:34).

In her book, *The Woman God Can Use,* Pamela Hoover Heim writes, "Because God forgets when He forgives, we can freely confess to Him as frequently as we must. Indeed, every time we sin, it is as if it were our first and only sin because if we have confessed all past disobediences, they have been thoroughly eradicated from the divine mind. We may confidently expect His mercy each time we need it."[17]

Since the consequences of our sins, or the sins of others, can continue to impact our lives as long as we live, we can't always forget sin completely the way God can. But we need to remove sin from the closets of our hearts by forgiving those who have sinned against us; by confessing our own sins; by forgiving ourselves; and by refusing to live in bondage to sin.

The only reason I have for dwelling on past sin at all is in order to share the good news that I have been forgiven—and you can be too.

A life free of the debris of unforgiven sin is not only a more peaceful life, it's also a healthier life, both mentally and physically.

In 1996, a study of thirty divorced mothers at the University of Wisconsin-Madison found that women who forgave their ex-husbands were less anxious and depressed, and became better parents, than those who could not forgive. (The study didn't mention their need to forgive themselves, but I have to believe that those who did scored even higher.) Other research has shown people who scored high on forgiveness scales had significantly lower levels of blood pressure, anxiety, and depression, and relatively high self-esteem.[18]

Forgiving sin can simplify our lives at the same time it makes us healthier. Certainly many doctor's appointments and counseling sessions are critical and unavoidable, but if we can just eliminate the ones necessitated by the effects of unforgiven sin, then we've successfully simplified our lives.

Calling on the power Jesus promises, simply forgive others. Forgive yourself. Put the hurt behind you. Go in peace.

CHAPTER 10

Simply Give

Freely you have received, freely give.
—Matthew 10:8

Two kinds of giving are integral to the simple life in Christ. First, we have to give of ourselves and our resources to others. Second, we have to give thanks to God.

How much simpler our lives would be if we freely gave away everything we didn't need. Why try to keep up with three pairs of gloves when we can only wear one at a time? By giving two pairs away, we can reduce the frustration by two-thirds!

The older I get the more I find I want to divest myself

of stuff. What better way to do that than to get into the habit of giving things away at every opportunity? It's one thing to give away the things we no longer need or want to charity, but real giving must go much further. I'd like to get to the point where if a dinner guest admires a plate or a goblet, I give it to her to take home. I'm not quite that liberated yet, but if a grandchild admires a candlestick, I do put a sticker with her name on the bottom so I know whom to give it to when it's time to downsize our household.

When my first granddaughter was born I had a very special necklace made to commemorate the event. It was a gold cross with a small diamond chip in the center. My plan was to wear it until she turned twenty-one, then give it to her as an heirloom.

When Francesca was just a baby, she'd reach for the cross around my neck, pull it to her mouth, and slobber all over it. As she got older, she'd sit on my lap and look for the chain so she could pull the cross out of my blouse and look at it.

"This is going to be my cross someday, isn't it, Grancy?" she would say. My heirloom-building plan was working beautifully. That is, until the summer before Francesca turned six. I had gone to visit her and her family. We were sightseeing in Creede, Colorado, when I realized my necklace was no longer around my neck. The safety clasp must have come undone. I was devastated.

"But that was supposed to be my cross, Grancy," Francesca said as we searched the sidewalks leading back to where the car was parked, and I thought my heart would break. When I saw that she was getting more upset each time she looked at my face, however, I realized I was sending her the wrong message. After all, the cross was special, but it was still just an object.

Finally, she and I sat down on a bench in front of a rustic general store in Creede. "I'll get another cross to give you, honey," I said.

"Will it have a diamond, Grancy?" she asked with excitement.

"No, I don't think so," I answered after some prompting from the Holy Spirit. "Now I know that you're my precious jewel, so I don't need one with a diamond. And you know what else? As long as we have each other, we shouldn't be so sad about losing the cross."

That talk and a couple of ice-cream cones made us both feel much better.

Driving home, I realized that my initial grief at losing the cross, and it did feel like grief, was not because of the value I placed on it, but because of how much I was looking forward to giving it to Francesca.

Paul quotes Jesus as having said, "'It is more blessed to give than to receive'" (Acts 20:35). We know that's true from the joy we experience in giving.

What's also true is that the more we give, the more blessed we are.

Always living a beautifully simple life, Mother Teresa gave her heart, mind, and soul to Jesus. In turn, she taught the Missionaries of Charity how to give in a way that would glorify Him. "I ask you one thing," she said. "Do not tire of giving, but do not give your leftovers. Give until it hurts, until you feel the pain."[19]

· · · · · ❖ · · · · ·

Giving thanks for our blessings each morning and each evening, and in all situations, keeps us from yearning for more than we have . . . more than we need.

· · · · · ❖ · · · · ·

Jesus didn't give us His leftovers. He gave us everything, and He did it willingly. When He speaks of laying down his life for His sheep in John 10:18, He says, "No one takes it from me, but I lay it down of my own accord."

We can't give as completely and unconditionally as

Jesus did, but we can make giving from our hearts a part of our lives each and every day, not just when it's convenient. And no matter how much we possess, we can always give.

No biblical account tells us more about Jesus' attitudes on giving than this story in Mark's Gospel. Jesus was watching what people were giving at the temple. He wasn't impressed when rich people threw in large amounts, but when He saw a widow put in two small coins, worth a fraction of a penny, He said to His disciples, "I tell you the truth, this poor widow has put more into the treasury than all the others. They all gave out of their wealth; but she, out of her poverty, put in everything—all she had to live on" (Mark 12:43-44).

Sometimes the poverty from which we are asked to give is emotional, not financial. On a hectic day at the office, with deadlines pending, do we give our time to the employee who obviously needs to talk? What about the tiny child pulling on our pant leg as we try to fix dinner? Can we give him the attention he deserves even if we're giving out of the poverty of exhaustion?

What are we willing to give in order to live a simple life that glorifies Him who gave His all? Before we can move beyond giving to giving until it hurts, we must have what Evelyn Christenson and others call an "attitude of gratitude" for all things and in all things.

"Thanksgiving is a life-style," Christenson wrote in *What Happens When God Answers Prayer.* "Our ultimate goal is to be engulfed by, saturated with, and completely controlled by an attitude of gratitude. Not some emotional high, or an escape from reality, but the actual living in a state of thankfulness—before, during and after we receive answers to our prayers."[20]

It's easy to be thankful for obvious blessings we receive, although we even take some of those for granted. What's harder is to give thanks as we are called to do in 1 Thessalonians 5:18; to "give thanks in all circumstances, for this is God's will for you in Christ Jesus."

My older son, Rob, and his family live in a one-stoplight town in southwest Colorado. His best friend, Vance, is the young pastor of a small congregation there. One day my son called and said he was driving up to meet Vance in Colorado Springs. Vance had been to Kansas in a borrowed flatbed truck to pick up an old tractor someone had given the church. The truck had broken down along the road, making it necessary for him to hitchhike to Colorado Springs to meet up with Rob.

I had about an hour's notice that the two young men were dropping in for lunch, but the Lord must have prepared the way because a big pot of homemade vegetable soup was simmering on the stove. (Not an everyday occurrence at our house, I assure you!) When they arrived,

Vance looked tired and dirty. After they washed up, the young pastor opened his heart to his Lord.

"Lord, thank You for that tractor," he prayed. "Thank You that You are going to get it to us. Right now, I don't know how that's going to happen, but I trust that You know, Lord. Thank You for all You are doing in my life and in the life of our church." How the tractor finally got to the church doesn't matter. God simply honored Vance's attitude of gratitude.

In her book *Simple Abundance,* Sarah Ban Breathnach suggests that those in search of the simple life keep their focus on what truly matters by keeping a gratitude journal, writing down at least five things for which to be grateful each day.[21] I think that's a wonderful idea. And whenever we make lists of things we're grateful to have, maybe we should also make lists of things we're grateful not to have. It doesn't take long to think of some—whether it's an incompetent boss or a sick child.

Even Jesus gave thanks. When He fed the five thousand with just five loaves and two small fish, we're told He "took the loaves, gave thanks, and distributed to those who were seated as much as they wanted" (John 6:11). At the Last Supper with His disciples, He "took bread, gave thanks and broke it, and gave it to them, saying, 'This is my body given for you; do this in remembrance of me'" (Luke 22:19).

As believers we have so very much, for we are inheritors of eternal glory! Giving freely of our earthly possessions and resources allows us to freely share the hope in our hearts as well. Giving thanks for our blessings each morning and evening, and in all situations, keeps us from yearning for more than we have . . . more than we need.

An oft-quoted Shaker hymn begins, " 'Tis a gift to be simple, 'Tis a gift to be free." We can have both simplicity and freedom when we know the blessings of giving to others, and of giving thanks to Him from whom we receive every good and perfect gift. "Give," He said, "and it will be given to you" (Luke 6:38).

CHAPTER 11

$\mathcal{S}$imply
$\mathcal{D}o$

I tell you the truth, anyone who has faith in me
will do what I have been doing.
—John 14:12

Most of us have more than enough "doing" in our lives already. Moving toward the simpler life means moving away from "doing" and toward "being" instead. How can we possibly add doing the things Jesus did to our to-do lists and still simplify?

It will only be possible with His help and with His editing of the things we've put on the list already. As Christians we are called to "Be doers of the word, and not hearers only" (James 1:22 NKJV). When we create our to-do lists from the Word, they include tasks like loving one another, encouraging one another, carrying one another's burdens, and serving one another . . . all as Jesus did.

"Jesus always gave people something to do," observes author Mike Murdock in his book, *The Leadership Secrets of Jesus.* "And, it was always something they had never done before. He knew that their obedience was the only proof of their faith in Him."[22]

A to-do list taken from the Word, and developed in consultation with Jesus, will contain far more relationship-building activities. There will be some self-improvement tasks, true, but only those that equip us to do the things He did in the world. Soon we'll notice that many of the things that once seemed so important aren't even making the list anymore, and far more things with eternal significance are.

Like the Apostle Paul, most of us are frustrated by the feeling that "what I want to do I do not do, but what I hate I do" (Romans 7:15). Any number of sins of omission or commission could come to mind as you read this verse. Personally, it always reminds me of procrastination—and of all the senseless things I do instead of doing something worthwhile. (Like watching television instead of reading the books I've purchased but not read.)

So what did Jesus do? First and always, He served others. He put people first. He prayed. He asked the Father to intervene. He listened. When our doing is similarly oriented, it won't seem impossible at all.

Imagine how the disciples must have felt when Jesus got down on His knees and proceeded to wash their feet. It was just before His death, and just after they had finally begun to understand that He truly was the Messiah; yet now He knelt before them as their servant.

When Jesus finished washing and drying the disciples' feet, He said, "Now that I, your Lord and Teacher, have washed your feet, you also should wash one another's feet. I have set you an example that you should do as I have done for you. I tell you the truth, no servant is greater than his master, nor is a messenger greater than the one who sent him. Now that you know these things, you will be blessed if you do them" (John 13:14-17).

Our service to others takes many forms. It seems impossible that doing for others could actually make life easier for us, but I've seen it happen time and time again. That's part of the blessing we're promised in the verses above.

Working as a corporate manager, I always had more in my in-basket than I could possibly do. Regular work hours were consumed by meetings, so deadline-oriented projects had to be done over lunch, early in the morning, or after hours. Inevitably, just when I was close to completing some important project, I would be interrupted by an employee asking for my time.

Time management experts might suggest I should have closed my door, or at least turned my back to the door to discourage intrusion. Should an employee interrupt, they would counsel, I would then be perfectly within my rights to suggest we get together at a time more convenient for me.

·····✣·····

Moving toward the simpler life means moving away from "doing" and toward "being" instead.

·····✣·····

But at some point on my pilgrimage I realized that if I wasn't in my job for the people, then nothing I was devoting my work life to had any meaning at all. I made a personal "people first" commitment, and I asked the Lord to honor it. He did.

I can't begin to enumerate the times when I returned to my work after a "people first" interruption with new insight that allowed me to finish more quickly. Other times, I received a phone call letting me know there had been an extension on the deadline I was dangerously close to missing. I received the blessing that came from doing what Jesus would do, and, contrary to standard logic, my life was made simpler at the same time.

Two verses sustained me during that period of my work life, and I kept them in sight on my tackboard or in my daily planner at all times. The first was, "Whatever you do, work at it with all your heart, as working for the Lord, not for men . . . It is the Lord Christ you are serving" (Col. 3:23-24). The second was Micah 6:8: "And what does the LORD require of you? To act justly and to love mercy and to walk humbly with your God." Just one glance at one of those verses on the most harried day would help me to regain my focus, take a deep breath, and proceed to do the next thing.

No matter how many business gurus claim to discover it, it was Jesus who first modeled the principle of leadership as service . . . and no one has ever demonstrated it more beautifully. Anyone in a leadership position is wise to look to Him as a mentor.

Serving others also includes hospitality. Jesus never had an earthly home, yet He had a way of making all kinds of people, even tiny children, feel welcome in His presence. That's the true meaning of hospitality: that others feel welcome in our presence. People feel welcome when they read in our eyes that we're glad to see them, hear the acceptance in our voices, and feel the warmth of our hugs.

(Want to increase the quality of your hugs? Don't be the first to let go.)

Being hospitable has everything to do with being available for another person and very little to do with setting the perfect dinner table or preparing the latest gourmet menu. Once we realize that truth, life and home entertaining both become simpler. Even if we just have people over for a great salad and a home-delivery pizza, they'll leave feeling royally entertained if we've made them feel as welcome in our presence as Jesus did the people He encountered.

"Do not forget to entertain strangers," the Bible says in Hebrews 13:2, "for by so doing some people have entertained angels without knowing it." What a gathering we could be missing! If we really want to do what Jesus would do, we wouldn't create guest lists based on whom we want to have over, or whom we need to pay back. Rather, we'd use Jesus' list.

"When you give a banquet," Jesus says, "invite the poor, the crippled, the lame, the blind, and you will be blessed" (Luke 14:13).

I was part of a group of women discussing this verse once when someone uncomfortably admitted, "You know, I don't even know any poor people, let alone have them over to dinner." I appreciated her candor, because it helped all of us realize not only how blessed we are, but also how far we are from Jesus' brand of hospitality. Because we haven't done what He would do in that realm, we haven't received the blessing He promises either.

We can't do everything Jesus did, but we can do something. Those who spend as much time as possible doing what Jesus would do have a peace about them regardless of the load of responsibility they carry.

In contrast, obsessively busy people living unfocused lives wear frantic faces, even if their busyness is motivated by the desire to do enough "good things" to guarantee their places in heaven.

Don't miss this point. We will *never* be able to do *anything* to earn our way to heaven. Our salvation is based on faith in Jesus Christ alone. It can be lived out through good deeds, sure, but it is guaranteed by faith. This knowledge allows us to mark all the "shoulds" off our lists and replace them with the "woulds"—as in "what would Jesus do?"

Once we do that, we may not wind up with fewer things on our to-do lists, but life will be simpler because the Lord of the Universe will be helping us do all things His way.

CHAPTER 12

Simply Abide

Abide in me, and I in you.
—John 15:4 KJV

For months we've had a small gray rabbit living in the overgrown juniper bush at the end of our driveway. Early in the morning, when I open the drapes in the living room to let the sun in, I see her sitting quietly in front of the bush nibbling on whatever little blades of green grass she can find.

Later in the day, I sometimes see her sunning herself in the same spot. When I walk across the lawn to collect the mail, the rabbit darts back into her bush, where she stays until she's ready to venture out again. If the golden retriever next door comes galumphing by, the rain pours down, or the winds howl, she just snuggles down in her burrow in the bush where she's safe from harm. The little rabbit abides in the bush. It is her home.

How Jesus longs for us to abide in Him in much the same way: to never venture too far without knowing how to get back to Him; to feel totally encompassed, and protected by Him at all times; to retreat to Him when the world seems too busy or too scary. Just simply to abide.

Abide is one of those words that seems old-fashioned in contemporary usage, yet its depth of meaning merits our reintroducing it into circles other than spiritual ones. To abide is to remain, stay, or tarry. To abide in Christ is to stay focused on Him, to be in intimate relationship with Him.

In John 15:4, Jesus says, "Abide in me, and I in you." With such abiding, there are no spaces in the togetherness between us and Him.

Andrew Murray, in his classic book *Abide in Christ*, points out that during His time on earth Jesus most often instructed his disciples to *follow* Him. "When about to leave for heaven," Murray writes, "He gave them a new word, in which their more intimate and spiritual union with Himself in glory should be expressed."[23] That new word was *abide*.

When we first fall in love we experience a feeling kin to abiding in another person even when he isn't present.

We are thinking of our beloved all the time, wishing he could see what we see . . . wishing we could share a thought even when we're apart. Jesus wants to be in relationship with us like that; to feel connected to everything we are doing, everything we are feeling, everything we are thinking. He promises to abide in us as we abide in Him.

How does abiding in Him make life simpler? How could it not? In Mark 4:37-41, we find an account of how calming it was for the disciples to be with Jesus. We read: "A furious squall came up, and the waves broke over the boat, so that it was nearly swamped. Jesus was in the stern, sleeping on a cushion. The disciples woke him and said to him, 'Teacher, don't you care if we drown?' He got up, rebuked the wind and said to the waves, 'Quiet! Be still!' Then the wind died down and it was completely calm."

When storms come crashing in on us today, He is still the only One who can command them to be still. Without Him, many people are left to bail for their lives, and yet the longer they bail, the higher the water rises.

I've noticed people playing a certain game for the last few years, a kind of one-upmanship that declares, "I'm busier than you are, so I must be more important than you are." Now with cell phones, fax machines attached to laptop computers in cars, and all the other communications technology we have, the game players have a lot more equipment with which to play.

Isn't it incredible that whereas we may have to pull out our daily planners to schedule a time to sit down and abide with Jesus, He'll be available anytime we choose? Excuse me, but the Lord of the Universe, who was present before Creation, is incredibly more important than we are; yet He never has to reschedule, and He never puts us on hold. If there's a game to be played, He has already won it.

· · · · · ❖ · · · · ·

When storms come crashing in on us today, Jesus is still the only One who can command them to be still.

· · · · · ❖ · · · · ·

We only have to look at a teenager doing his homework while listening to music on a headset, watching TV, checking e-mail, and talking on the phone all at the same time to realize how conditioned our society is to avoiding solitude. But we need to learn how to be alone, without any of the world's clamor to keep us entertained, so that we can be with Jesus and hear the still, quiet voice of the Holy Spirit.

In order to abide with Him we must seek Him in the calm of our hearts. So many people love to spend quiet time with the Lord in the early morning before the demands and noises of the day begin, just so they can experience the joy of quietly abiding in Him. Whenever we invite Him to join us, He will, because He's already there abiding inside us.

One of the hardest things for me to adjust to when I started working at home was being alone in a quiet house all day. I know mothers of young children will be thinking, "I'd give up my last fast-food coupon for just one day at home alone," and I understand how they feel. But as an empty-nester and an extrovert, I miss the busyness of a full house and the interaction that comes from being part of a team-oriented work group. No one is here during the day except our two cats, and they really don't want me interrupting their busy nap schedule.

The positive thing about my new life, however, is that I can calmly turn to the Lord any time I want. He's always here, and because of Him, I'm never lonely or alone.

Richard Foster writes, "Simplicity and solitude walk hand in hand."[24] Certainly, it's easier to live a simple life when you have solitude. "Withdraw yourself from all needless distraction," Andrew Murray suggests, "close your ears to the voices of the world, and be as a docile learner, ever listening for the heavenly wisdom the Master has to teach."[25]

Walking outdoors—preferably through a garden—is

an excellent way to withdraw with Jesus. Adam and Eve walked with God in the cool of the day. It was in the Garden of Gethsemane where Jesus went to pray, abiding in solitude with His heavenly Father before His arrest and persecution.

Gardens hold so many special memories for me. Even a hymn about a garden makes me smile! One of my grandmothers lived with us while I was growing up, so she always kept my sisters and me whenever our parents went out. On one of those Saturday evenings, after we'd had our baths, I remember Granny gathering us around her old piano to sing hymns. I can still see the smile in her eyes when she gave us the nod to join in on the chorus of "In the Garden." It went like this: "And . . . He . . . walks with me, and He talks with me, and He tells me I am His own. And the joy we share as we tarry there, none other has ever known."[26]

You know the Master of the wind. Invite Him to go for a walk. Tell Him you love Him. Praise Him for all He is doing in your life. Ask Him questions about anything you don't understand. Give Him your mental lists of things to do, and listen as He tells you His eternal priorities.

Simply abide in Him, and He will abide in you.

CHAPTER 13

Simply Let Go

Jesus looked at them and said,
"With man this is impossible, but not with God;
all things are possible with God."
—Mark 10:27

The rich young ruler came to Jesus in all earnestness and asked Him what it would take to have eternal life. The Gospel of Mark tells us Jesus looked at him and loved him, but He also saw how important the young man's wealth was to him. That's why Jesus told him, "Go, sell everything you have and give to the poor, and you will have treasure in heaven" (Mark 10:21).

The disciples were amazed by Jesus' answer. Even

though they had left everything to follow Jesus, they didn't see how a man so wealthy could be expected to give up so much. Jesus understood their worldly perspective. That's why He said, "With man this is impossible; but not with God; all things are possible with God" (Mark 10:27).

Does Jesus want us to live in comfortable homes? Does He want our children to have clothes to wear and food to eat? Does He want us to succeed in our work? He may or may not, depending on His plan for our lives. Regardless, He asks that we resist the temptation to hold onto anything or anyone more tightly than we hold to our desire to love, obey, and follow Him.

A friend of mine who lost her mother at an early age has struggled with materialism most of her adult life. She has also struggled with letting go of her adult children. As she approached her fiftieth birthday, she said, "I think I'm finally understanding what the Lord wants of me. He's telling me it's okay for me to love all that I have, as long as I hold it all loosely."

I believe learning to hold everything loosely is the key not only to keeping our possessions and relationships in eternal perspective, but also to simplifying our lives. If we accept that all things are from God and belong to God, and that He can ask us to give up anything at any time, then we free ourselves from frantically trying to hold on to everything and everyone within our grasp.

Every so often, I take a mental inventory of my life to see if there is any job, relationship, or attitude that I'm holding on to with my fingers tightly clinched. If there is, I pray for the strength to hold it more loosely—or to let it go entirely. After all, I want to keep my hands empty. If they are already full, they won't be free to give or to receive.

To live a simpler life we must let go of our desire to acquire.

· · · · · ❖ · · · · ·

To live a simpler life,
we must let go of our desire to acquire.

· · · · · ❖ · · · · ·

"Possession is an obsession in our culture," Richard Foster writes. "If we own it we feel that we can control it; and if we control it, we feel that it will give us more plea-sure. The idea is an illusion."[27] Citing libraries, schools, and parks as examples, Foster suggests we can learn to enjoy things without possessing them.

We also need to let go of trying to control every situa-tion. For instance, women working outside the home can find tremendous peace by letting go of the need to com-pete. I know this sounds radical. I'm a product of the 70s and 80s and I realize how hard women fought for equal pay and equal opportunity. Still, I have come to accept that God wants me to use my talents and skills to the best of my own ability, and to glorify Him, not to compete with other women—or with men. Letting go of the need to compete won't affect your ability to achieve, but it will change your life. It will also save an incredible amount of energy—energy you can use someplace else.

Next, we need to let go of our desire to fix everything. Remember the poem about the little girl who brought a broken toy to the Lord to fix, but was disappointed when it still didn't work? She asked Him why He didn't fix it. His response was that He couldn't, because she didn't give Him all the pieces.

So often we want to fix things and people ourselves, without giving any of the pieces to Him. This is especially true of our children. How desperately we want to make the world a welcoming, accepting place for them and spare them the pain life can inflict.

The letting go process for parents begins the first day the oldest child makes his way to the bus stop, his oversized backpack bouncing along behind him, and it doesn't end until the last child is on her own. (Even then, fear of the empty nest motivates many of us to try to keep holding on, much to the detriment of our children's independence and our own serenity.)

I didn't let go of one of my sons until the Lord tore him out of my hands. Perhaps due to the divorce, his unique makeup, or both, he had an extremely trying adolescence. No matter how much I prayed he would stay in high school, he dropped out three times. I was always ready to pick up the pieces and find a solution for him. Later I learned my efforts to fix things really just enabled and prolonged his rebellion.

One night I cried myself to sleep over what to do next. (Not an uncommon thing for a single mom to do.) When I awoke, I had the feeling the Lord was shaking me, then that He was throwing me into a chair in the corner of my bedroom. "Please let go of that boy!" He said sternly. "I can't do a thing with him until you let go."

I did let go, and the consequences were not all good. Yet the Lord was faithful, and used the path He had chosen, not the one I thought best, to bring my son into full, productive adulthood. Today he's a college graduate, a business owner, and a loving, Christian husband and father.

When we really trust that our lives, and the lives of our children, are in the Lord's hands, we can let go. As the prophet Isaiah said to the Lord, "We are the clay, you are the potter" (Isaiah 64:8). Imagine an artist at work shaping a lump of clay on a potter's wheel. If someone else walks up and grabs hold of the clay while the artist is working, the intended design will be ruined, and the artist will be frustrated. That must be how the Lord feels when we interfere with His design for the people we love.

We must also let go of our fear if we are to live a simple life of faith. Jesus knows fear and faith can't coexist, so He says, "Do not let your hearts be troubled and do not be afraid" (John 14:27). How comforting it is to read those words and the ones in the Gospel of Luke: "Do not be afraid, little flock, for your Father has been pleased to give you the kingdom" (Luke 12:32).

An attitude of surrender precedes our ability to let go in faith. "There is only one thing God wants of us, and that is our absolute surrender," Oswald Chambers writes.[28] "There must be a surrender of the will, not a surrender to persuasive power, a deliberate launching forth on God and on what He says until I am no longer confident in what I have done, I am confident only in God."[29]

God wants us to act confidently and responsibly, but He also wants us to acknowledge that our best efforts are only as good as our dependence on Him.

How do we let go on a practical, everyday basis? Often it's by asking in prayer for the attitude of surrender. It's also by asking, "Am I in control of this, or is God?" A friend of mine finds it helps her to give up her fears and worries if she writes them on small pieces of paper, which she puts in a jar on a shelf too high to reach easily. I like to envision taking a situation and laying it at the foot of the cross where Jesus wants us to leave all our worldly cares. "Come to me, all you who are weary and burdened, and I will give you rest," Jesus says (Matt. 11:28). He wants us to let go of all our burdens and cast them on Him . . . every single one of them.

As difficult as it is, we even need to be ready to let go of life itself, and to say with the Apostle Paul, "For to me, to live is Christ and to die is gain" (Phil. 1:21). Noted missionary Jim Elliot did this when his life was threatened by the Quichua Indians in South America. Just before he and his co-workers were massacred by the very people they had come to help, Elliot said, "He is no fool who gives what he cannot keep to gain what he cannot lose."[30] Like Paul, Elliot knew his real treasures were in heaven, not in the flesh.

Of course, Jesus modeled the ultimate surrender for us when He said from the cross, "Father, into your hands I commit my spirit" (Luke 23:46). When we can simply let go we will be free. Jesus promises us that with God, it is possible.

$\mathscr{S}$imply $\mathscr{F}ollow$

I am the light of the world.
Whoever follows me will never walk in darkness,
but have the light of life.
—John 8:12

Each year thousands of Christians go on a spiritual pilgrimage to the Holy Land. Drawing on their life's savings to finance the trip, they venture out to see with their own eyes the valleys and mountains that Jesus saw when He walked on earth. They want to stroll along the shores of the Sea of Galilee, then board a boat and sail to Capernaum just as He did. They yearn to climb the Mount of Beatitudes and imagine what it was like to be part of the crowd sitting at Jesus' feet when He said, "Blessed are those who hunger and thirst for righteousness, for they will be filled" (Matt. 5:6).

Yet as inspiring and wonderful as a trip to the Holy Land is, it isn't necessary for us to physically follow in Jesus' steps down the well-worn stones of the Via Dolorosa in order to follow Him. It's only necessary for us to be ready to go wherever He calls us; to adopt a simple posture of readiness in spite of all our responsibilites, relationships, and possessions.

The Gospels are peppered with Jesus' encounters with people whom He invited to simply follow Him. Strolling beside the Sea of Galilee, Jesus encountered Simon, later called Peter, and his brother Andrew casting their fishing nets into the water. "Come, follow me," He said, "and I will make you fishers of men" (Matt. 4:19). The Gospel recounts their response as a simple one. "At once they left their nets and followed him" (Matt. 4:20).

Matthew had the same response when Jesus saw him sitting at the tax collector's booth. "Follow me, he told him, and Matthew got up and followed him" (Matt. 9:9).

Those who followed Jesus on earth responded to His simple call only if they could quickly become unencumbered. Just as the rich, young ruler in the Gospel of Mark didn't follow Jesus because he was clinging to his wealth, we sometimes fail to follow Him as quickly and as enthusiastically as He deserves because we are clinging to something too tightly.

Reading the Gospel of Mark from beginning to end, I began to get caught up emotionally and viscerally in the increasing momentum of Jesus' ministry and His message. It must not have been easy to follow Him the last year or so, for as the time drew nearer for Him to return to the Father, his travel schedule grew intentionally more demanding as his teaching grew more intense.

To follow Him and keep up with His agenda, the disciples had to travel light. So do we. "Simplicity is part and parcel of our call to be a disciple of Jesus Christ," Richard Foster writes. "It is not an 'extra' that we can tack onto our Christian experience."[31]

Pilgrims to the Holy Land, and those who only dream of going, need to remember that they can still follow Jesus as surely as those who saw His footprints in the sand. For even those blessed to live in close fellowship with Him at the time God chose for Him to become flesh and walk among us could not follow Him physically.

"Where I am going, you cannot follow now, but you will follow later," Jesus says (John 13:36). Jesus wanted His disciples to understand that the only way they could be with Him forever was to join Him on His mission. They were to follow Him by doing what He asked them to do in the world. In that regard, we have the very same opportunity that the disciples had as long as we maintain a simple position of readiness.

·····✤·····

When He calls you, simply follow.

·····✤·····

Like those who gazed into Jesus' eyes and heard His voice, we can follow Him if we're willing to at least emotionally free ourselves of any and every encumbrance. Even if we become afraid that we can't keep up, or can't see where Jesus is leading us, we still need to keep following. Out of our faithfulness to keep following even through our uncertainty, Oswald Chambers writes, "will come that following of Jesus which is an unspeakable joy"[32]

Like a ski instructor who turns to make sure the class of six year olds is trailing her safely down the mountain, Jesus always looks around to make sure we are still following Him. When necessary, He'll wait for us to catch up.

What slows us down? Perhaps it's not the baggage the world hands us at all. Perhaps it's the very weight of our discipleship.

In the Gospel of Matthew Jesus says, "If anyone wants to be a follower of mine, let him deny himself and take up his cross and follow me" (Matt.16:24 TLB). Our crosses aren't literally the ones the disciples had reason to fear were in their futures; yet if we are to remain followers of Jesus Christ, we must daily die to self and pick up the cross of obedience to Him no matter what persecution we might face.

I wasn't there when Peter and Andrew tossed aside their nets after Jesus said, "Follow me"; yet I've seen others respond to that same command, and I've responded to it myself.

When Jesus left the world, He sent the Holy Spirit to dwell in the hearts of believers. That's why the command "Follow me" often begins as a whisper from deep inside us. Once we hear the whisper, we should drop everything and respond immediately. More likely, we think of a hundred reasons why we can't.

I was working full time in a management position when I began to feel a persistent yearning to go home— not for the day, for good! Through prayer, I began to understand that the yearning was really a message from the Holy Spirit.

"Why, Lord?" I asked repeatedly. "Why should I go home now when my children are grown and gone and there is no one at home during the day who needs me?"

"Trust me," the Spirit seemed to say. "I have other things for you to do."

A co-worker of mine struggled for years in a web of guilt. She felt guilty when she was at work because she wasn't at home with her two little boys, and she felt guilty when she was at home because she wasn't getting everything done at work. It's a conundrum most working mothers experience, whether they admit it or not; one made more difficult for my friend Cathy because she was doing an excellent job in her challenging marketing position.

After months of agonizing indecision, she told me one day with tears in her eyes that she had decided to listen to her heart and cut back to part-time. A few months later, she quit her job entirely and started a marketing consulting business from her home. We had lunch recently, and I've never seen Cathy looking more beautiful or happier. (It's amazing how much better we look without the dark circles under our eyes and furrowed brows, isn't it?)

Of course not all of the heart messages we receive have to do with work-related issues. The Spirit speaks to us on all topics at all times. What some label intuition or insight is to the believer simply the voice of the Spirit delivering the message from Jesus: "Come, follow me."

Once we begin the journey, once we hear His call and follow in His footsteps whether on the shores of the Sea of Galilee or the sidewalk outside our house, there's no turning back. We must continue to "walk in the light as He is in the light" (1 John 1:7).

"Do you continue to go with Jesus?" Oswald Chambers asks. "The way lies through Gethsemane, through the city gate, outside the camp; the way lies alone, and the way lies until there is no trace of a footstep left, only the voice, 'Follow me.'"[33]

Jesus says, "Whoever follows me will never walk in darkness, but will have the light of life" (John 8:12). When He calls you, simply follow.

CHAPTER 15

Simply Love

*As I have loved you,
so you must love one another.*
—John 13:34

Simply believing in Jesus as God's holy Son is the first step to simplifying our lives through Him. Simply loving Him because He first loved us, and continues to love us unconditionally, is what makes it possible for us to keep simplification a life-long priority. It's so much easier to trust Him, to listen to Him, and to abide in Him when we simply love Him.

"God is love," we read in the first Epistle of John. "Whoever lives in love lives in God, and God in him"

(1 John 4:16). Since Jesus is God incarnate, God in the flesh, He too is love. When God sent Jesus to dwell with us, He was sending us love. "For God so loved the world that He gave his one and only Son, that whoever believes in him shall not perish but have eternal life" (John 3:16). No gift, no love, will ever be greater.

It is our simple, uncomplicated response to God's love for us that brings joy and simplicity to our journey. God cares about our response just as anyone who loves longs for reciprocal love.

"God pursues a continuing love relationship with you that is real and personal," Henry Blackaby reminds each of us.[34] In other words, God goes out of His way to let us know how much He loves us.

Here's how I know God loves me. He loves me so much that even if I were the only person on earth He would still have sent Jesus to die for me so that I could dwell in His presence for eternity. He loves me enough to convict me of my sins and free me from even the guilt of them. He loves me enough to indwell me with the Holy Spirit to comfort and guide me. He loves me enough to give me people to love and be loved by, work to do, and a Creation to explore. All the theologians in the world couldn't come up with a more profound statement than the words of the children's song: "Jesus loves me, this I know, for the Bible tells me so." I know He loves me, and I know He loves you too.

Life is difficult for those who fail to accept God's love for them. "Very few people know that they are loved without any conditions or limits," Henri Nouwen wrote. "This unconditional and unlimited love is what the evangelist John calls God's first love. 'Let us love,' he says, 'because God first loved us' (1 John 4:19)."[35]

Jesus tells us how to respond to such an Almighty love when He says, "'Love the Lord your God with all your heart and with all your soul and with all your mind.' This is the first and greatest commandment. And the second is like it: 'Love your neighbor as yourself'" (Matt. 22:37-39).

We must love God and we must love ourselves. If we don't love ourselves, will we truly be able to love our neighbors, our spouses, and our children? It's not likely. Until we understand how much God loves us, we don't feel lovable or significant. Once we fully accept His love, however, then we are able to reach out to others.

St. Francis of Assisi built his life of service on his view of God's love. "With all our hearts and souls, all our minds and all our strength, all our understanding, with every faculty and every effort, with every affection and all our emotions, with every wish and every desire, we should love our Lord and God who gives us everything, body and soul, and all our life; it was he who created and redeemed us and of his mercy alone he will save us."[36]

Surely no one in this century exemplified reaching out to others with simple love more than did Mother Teresa of Calcutta. In the Apostle Paul's letter to the Galatians, he wrote, "the only thing that counts is faith expressing itself through love" (Gal. 5:6). Mother Teresa's life was a testimony to her belief that love and faith went hand in hand. She endeavored to love everyone God put before her and to see Jesus in every face.

· · · · · ❖ · · · · ·

It is our simple, uncomplicated response to God's love for us that brings joy and simplicity to our journey

· · · · · ❖ · · · · ·

"God has created us to do small things with great love," Mother Teresa said. "I believe in that great love, that comes, or should come from the heart, should start at home: with my family, my neighbors across the street, those right next door. And this love should then reach everyone."[37]

To the extent we can also take God's love to the poor,

the homeless, and the downtrodden, we will be blessed. But even without such generous gifts of our resources and time, love can simplify and enrich our lives.

Within our marriage relationships, do we have to get our own way or do we simply love? When faced with an adversarial situation at work or home, do we struggle to stay in control or do we simply love? Jesus says we should even love our enemies and pray for those who persecute us (Matt. 5:44). He doesn't say this so that life will take unfair advantage of us, but so the world will see His love through us. When His love is put into the center of any conflict, the problem is often resolved more quickly.

Perhaps no relationship we have comes closer to the unconditional love God has for us than does the love of a parent for a child. Not only can we understand God's love and sacrifice for us more deeply when we relate it to our own love for our children, but the parent-child relationship is also one of our best opportunities to pass on the love we have been given.

I was reminded of this truth when my son Tim's first child was born. I didn't get to see little Ellie until she was almost three weeks old. Before I met her and got to feel her little head snuggled under my chin as we rocked, Tim was wonderful about calling regularly with updates.

For years I've ended phone conversations with my sons by saying, "I love you." More than just a perfunctory close to the conversation, my expression of love is a way of making sure that if anything ever happens to me or to them, we won't have to wish we had shared our feelings. Besides, it is so important for even grown children to receive the blessing of their parents, and saying "I love you" is a part of that blessing.

One of the times Tim called after Ellie's birth, he held the baby in the crook of his arm as we talked. I could hear her little baby noises as she looked up at her dad and he gazed down at her. Suddenly Tim said, "I love you, Mom," before I had a chance to say it to him, and I heard in his voice a dimension of love that hadn't been there before. Now that he knew the love of a parent for a child, the love my mother still gives me, he more fully understood my love for him. Loving Ellie had given him the ability to receive and return love more richly than ever before.

How blessed all of us in God's family are to have His love flowing through us to those we love, and even to those we may pass on the street. We never know when a smile or a kind word from us will give someone in despair just enough of God's gracious love to get them through the day.

We simply love because He first loved us. Love so simple . . . love so profound. The more we know Jesus, the more we know His heart, and the more we love Him. The more we love Him, the more we will want to obey Him, and the more He will be able to accomplish His work through us. "Whoever has my commands and obeys them, he is the one who loves me," Jesus says (John 14:21).

In the Gospel of John, chapter twenty-one, we read that Jesus asked Peter if he loved Him three times. Twice He used the Greek word *agape*, meaning volitional, self-sacrificing love, and once He used the word *phileo*, signifying affection or brotherly love. He wanted to be sure of Peter's complete love, and He wanted Peter to come to terms with his real feelings for Him.

Just as Jesus still asks us if we believe in Him, the question He asked Martha on the road outside of her house, so He still asks us the question He asked Peter: "Do you love me?" His love for us is so perfect, so complete, so forgiving, so all-encompassing, how can our reply be anything besides, "Yes, Lord, you know that I love you" (John 21:16)?

To simply love Him is to open our hearts and allow His love to flow through us to others. It is simply the Savior who gives us all the love and all the power we need to live a life of simple joy.

> *Grace to all who love our Lord Jesus Christ*
> *with an undying love.*
> —Ephesians 6:24

Endnotes

1. C. S. Lewis, *Mere Christianity*, (New York: Macmillan Publishing Company, 1952), 41.
2. Richard J. Foster, *Freedom of Simplicity*, (New York: Harper & Row, 1981), 34.
3. Henri J. Nouwen, *In the Name of Jesus*, (New York: Crossroad, 1989), 23.
4. Ibid., 60.
5. Stephen R. Covey, *The 7 Habits of Highly Effective People*, (New York: Simon & Schuster, 1989), 157.
6. Ibid., 156.
7. Henry T. Blackaby & Claude V. King, *Experiencing God*, (Nashville, Tennessee: The Sunday School Board of the Southern Baptist Convention, 1990), 83.
8. Barbara K. Mouser, *Five Aspects of Woman: A Biblical Theology of Femininity*, (Waxahachie, Texas: International Council for Gender Studies, 1995), 1.19.
9. Mother Teresa, *Mother Teresa In My Own Words*, comp. José Luis González-Balado (New York: Random House, 1997), 94.
10. Oswald Chambers, *My Utmost for His Highest*, (Westwood, New Jersey: Barbour and Company, Inc.,1963), 226.
11. Linda Dillow, "Why Should I Trust God?," *Discipleship Journal*, January/February 1998, 44.
12. E. B. White, *Essays of E.B. White* (New York: Harper & Row, 1977), 4.

13. Steve Laube, "A Writer's Folly," Glorieta Christian Writers Conference, 9 November 1997.

14. Foster, *Freedom of Simplicity*, 127.

15. © 1997 Allstate Insurance Company, Northbrook, IL.

16. Mary A. White, *Harsh Grief, Gentle Hope*, (Colorado Springs, Colorado: Navpress, 1995),13.

17. Pamela Hoover Heim, *The Woman God Can Use*, (Denver, Colorado: Accent, 1986), 54.

18. David Briggs, Associated Press, "Forgiveness All the Vogue," *The Denver Post*, 20 December 1997, 30A.

19. Mother Teresa, *Mother Teresa In My Own Words*, 17.

20. Evelyn Christenson, *What Happens When God Answers Prayer*, (Colorado Springs, Colorado: Chariot Victor, 1986, 1994), 184.

21. Sarah Ban Breathnach, *Simple Abundance*, (New York: Warner Books, 1995), January 14.

22. Mike Murdock, *The Leadership Secrets of Jesus*, (Tulsa, Oklahoma: Honor Books, 1996), 125.

23. Andrew Murray, *Abide in Christ*, (Springdale, Pennsylvania: Whitaker House, 1979), 5.

24. Foster, *Freedom of Simplicity*, 12.

25. Murray, *Abide in Christ*, 54.

26. "In the Garden," ©1940, The Rodeheaver Co.

27. Foster, *Freedom of Simplicity*, 143.

28. Chambers, *My Utmost for His Highest*, 297.

29. Ibid., 357.

30. Elisabeth Elliot, *Shadow of the Almighty, The Life and Testament of Jim Elliot* (New York: Harper & Brothers Publishers, 1958), 247.

31. Foster, *Freedom of Simplicity*, 183.

32. Chambers, *My Utmost for His Highest*, 75.
33. Ibid., 263.
34. Blackaby & King, *Experiencing God*, 20.
35. Nouwen, *In the Name of Jesus*, 25.
36. St. Francis of Assisi, *The Writings of St. Francis of Assisi*, trans. Benen Fahy, O. F. M. (Chicago: Franciscan Herald Press, 1963), 51.
37. Mother Teresa, *Mother Teresa In My Own Words*, 45.